THOUGHTS RULE THE WORLD

TO

> . . . *the seeker of truth*
> . . . *the exemplar of liberty:*
> *the key to a better world!*, including

a great freedom devotee,

Frank

all my best!

Leonard

LEONARD E. READ

THOUGHTS RULE THE WORLD

The Foundation for Economic Education, Inc.
Irvington-on-Hudson, New York 10533
1981

THE AUTHOR AND PUBLISHER

Leonard E. Read has been president of The Foundation for Economic Education since it was organized in 1946.

The Foundation is a nonpolitical, nonprofit, educational institution. Its senior staff and numerous writers are students as well as teachers of the free market, private ownership, limited government rationale. Sample copies of the Foundation's monthly study journal, *The Freeman,* are available on request.

Published January 1981

ISBN-0-910614-67-9

CONTENTS

1. THOUGHTS RULE THE WORLD   1

    The spiritual origin of all by which we live and pros-
    per.

2. FREEDOM IS NOT FREE   5

    Each generation must earn it.

3. PRE-EMPTION: LEGAL THIEVERY   10

    Stop asking government to steal for you!

4. GOOD INTENTIONS GONE ASTRAY   16

    The end pre-exists in the means.

5. WOE BETIDE YE OF LITTLE TRUST   22

    Freedom comes to those who trust one another.

6. LITTLE MEN CAUSE BIG GOVERNMENT   26

    Bondage for those who fail to try.

7. GOODNESS: THE FIRST STEP TO FREEDOM   30

    Not in outward things but in the inward thing we are.

8. DEPENDENCE AND INDEPENDENCE   34

   Cooperation among self-reliant individuals.

9. THE FREE MIND   39

   Accountable to a higher tribunal than man's.

10. LOVE MAKES THE WORLD GO ROUND   44

    We are shaped and fashioned by what we love.

11. THE PRACTICE OF MANNERS AND MORALS   48

    These twin virtues are signs of maturity.

12. WHY THE PRESIDENT SAID NO   53

    In defense of limited government.

13. OBLIGATIONS SPAWN MENTAL GROWTH   58

    Obstacles as steppingstones.

14. OUR MUTUAL OBLIGATIONS   62

    Learning is a sharing of ideas.

15. THE ROLE OF GOALS   66

    Not failure, but low aim is crime.

16. THE VOICE OF CONSCIENCE   69

    Conscience asks, is it right?

17. THE EMERGENCE OF TRUTH   73

    The more one knows, the greater the unknown.

18. ASPIRE TO SEE AFAR   76

Genius is a superior power of seeing.

19. FROM THE ''KNOWN'' TO THE UNKNOWN   81

Each achievement reveals a higher goal.

20. THE MASTERS OF VICTORY   86

Those with the wisdom, courage, and determination
to win.

21. THE POWER OF THINKING JOYOUSLY   90

Take comfort in achievement.

22. THOUGHTS: DEAD OR ALIVE?   95

Ideas are powerless unless activated.

23. COUNT OUR BLESSINGS, NOT MISERIES   99

Enjoy thine own, envy not others.

24. REAPING THE BLESSINGS OF FREEDOM   105

Those who would expect to reap the blessings of
freedom must undergo the fatigue of supporting it.

25. PERFECTION? KNOWING OUR
IMPERFECTIONS   109

Those most assume who know the least.

26. GOOD NEWS   115

Individuals best help themselves and others when
free.

INDEX   119

1

THOUGHTS RULE THE WORLD

Great men are they who see that spiritual is stronger than material force, that thoughts rule the world. **—EMERSON**

Discoveries, inventions, insights, intuitive flashes—thoughts—are what I understand by "spiritual." It is obvious that *everything* by which we live and prosper has its origin in the spiritual before its manifestation in the material. First the ideas, then the object. One of the countless examples: To claim that my electric typewriter is the product of a million thoughts would be a gross understatement. Reflect on these points:

- Press the button and instantly electric energy flows. No one can come close to estimating the number of thoughts that have contributed to this phenomenon—from the day Benjamin Franklin with his kite discovered that lightning is electricity to today's electronic miracles!
- That which encases all of this fantastic gadgetry originates from a combination of mined ore. Modern mining includes everything from ropes to shovels to elevators to dynamite to

1

consumer demand. Thoughts galore, beyond anyone's imagination, no two identical!

• Facing the typist are 55 keys, the touching of which performs a magical function. Of what are these gadgets made? Millions of thoughts! And reflect on the letters, from A to Z, components of the English language. Who can calculate the number of thoughts that brought them into being over the centuries? No one, even remotely!

The above paragraphs have to do only with the thoughts responsible for the creation of a typewriter. Imagine how many more thoughts it has taken to account for the automobile! Every day for the past 80 years new thoughts have added improvements to the vehicle we take for granted. A 747 Jet has 5,000,000 parts and no individual knows how to make a single one of them—any more than anyone knows how to make a simple wooden lead pencil.[1]

I glance around my office and see at least a hundred items, ranging from beautiful artificial flowers to an accurate radio-clock. No one knows how to make a single one of these items, or even the pen I use as I ponder the complexities of the role of thought!

The point is that no one person has the capacity to manage the storm of thoughts that bombard the universe. But when free to flow, thoughts tend to configurate into the goods and services by which we live and prosper. So, let us have faith in freedom.

Given a sufficient realization that thoughts are fleeting, ever-changing, in an ideological flurry—given this understanding—the practice and impact of know-it-all-ness would dwindle. When it is recognized that no person on this earth—past or present—

---

[1] See "I, Pencil," copy on request.

can command the thoughts of a single individual, let alone the millions, the command way of life is seen to be the mistaken way of the past. Politicians will be replaced by statesmen; our 78,000 governments—federal, state and local—will be limited to prohibiting the acts of aggression and destruction of a disappearing number of wiseacres. The cost of all governments will be insignificant—this alone being worth the ideological struggle.

Good thinkers of our day are blest with thoughts by wise men the world over, from ancient to modern times. Examples: Confucius, Socrates, Jesus, Epictetus, John Locke, Edmund Burke, Bastiat, Cobden, Bright, Adam Smith, Washington, Emerson and many more.

This good advice from the Roman Emperor and philosopher, Marcus Aurelius (121-180): "The happiness of your life depends upon the quality of your thoughts, therefore guard accordingly; and take care that you entertain no notions unsuitable to virtue." Aurelius was a devoted Stoic who held to the philosophy that all happenings are the result of Divine Will. Thus, no belief, none whatsoever, in a political or any other type of dictocrat!

That happiness depends on the quality of our thoughts is a truism. Wrote the French philosopher, Blaise Pascal (1623-62): "Happiness is neither within us only, or without us; it is a union of ourselves with God." As to quality of thought, this is unquestionably *number one!*

Aurelius wisely cautions against notions unsuitable to virtue. Briefly, entertain no thoughts nor take any actions out of harmony with Judeo-Christian charity, intelligence, justice, integrity, love, humility, reverence!

The elderly American divine, Daniel March (1816-1919) gave us this bit of wisdom: "The great thinker is seldom a disputant. He answers other men's arguments by stating the truth as he sees it.'' In our realm of thought, the freedom devotee who trades blows with a socialist merely hardens the latter in his ways. Bad method! Stating the truth of freedom, when done with enough expertise, occasionally attracts a socialist to a better idea. Good method!

Truly, thoughts rule the world. However, their rule will never be to mankind's benefit unless the most difficult thought of all is understood and practiced. And what might that be? Several benchmarks:

1. To concede that everything is mystery, that is, to realize how infinitesimal is your or my understanding.
2. To recognize that trillions times trillions of good thoughts— no two alike—when left free to flow, will *mysteriously configurate* to the benefit of one and all as we stand in worshipful wonder.
3. ''I call that mind free which protects itself against the usurpations of society, which does not cower to human opinions, which feels itself accountable to a higher tribunal than man's.''

William Ellery Channing

He or she who stands in reverence of Creation is indeed *one whom the truth makes free!*

*   *   *

In the conviction that thoughts rule the world, I offer this, my 27th book. More accurately, it is a series of essays—thoughts on freedom as they have come to mind—enclosed between two covers.

2

FREEDOM IS NOT FREE

*Those who deny freedom to oth-
ers deserve it not for themselves.* **—ABRAHAM LINCOLN**

Only a few—the pure, the apt and the true—never deny freedom
to anyone. All others, while they may hope for freedom for
themselves, deny this blessing to others in countless ways, sometimes knowingly but often in ignorance. Whoever diminishes
your freedom deserves it not for himself! Thanks, Honest Abe!

We can also thank William Harvard for his counsel: "The
greatest glory of a free-born people is to transmit that freedom to
their children." Never in all history were a people more blest in
being freeborn than Americans. And for at least twelve decades
they transmitted this blessing to their children. Then came the
slump and for many reasons, ranging from prosperity going to
their heads—thinking gone dormant—to government "education."

Lincoln's thought reversed would read: When enough of us
grant freedom to others we shall have it for ourselves! For, as
Edmund Burke wrote: "Depend on it, the lovers of freedom will
be free."

5

Who amongst us have the capability or the potentiality of advancing an understanding of freedom? Only those individuals who find the freedom cause a happy pursuit. Wrote Saint Augustine about sixteen centuries ago: "Happiness consists in the attainment of our desires and in our having only right desires." Among the right desires is freedom!

If we are to enjoy the blessings of freedom, there are ever so many ideas and ideals that must grace our understanding and exposition. Among these are (1) the proper role of government and (2) the rights of citizens. According to the late Robert H. Jackson, Justice of the Supreme Court from 1941 to 1945: "It is not the function of government to keep the citizens from error; it is the function of citizens to keep the government from falling into error."

Wrote the Roman Emperor and philosopher, Marcus Aurelius Antoninus (121–180), "Our understandings are always liable to error. Nature and certainty are very hard to come at, and infallibility is mere vanity and pretense." A very large percentage of elected and appointed officials assume they are infallible and, as a consequence, attempt to protect us from our countless errors. The costs of this assumed infallibility? Almost without limit. For one, inflation on the rampage! As the Bard of Avon wrote, "You take my life when you take the means by which I live."

Now to the important side of this problem. Justice Robert H. Jackson pronounced a great truth: *"It is the function of citizens to keep the government from falling into error."* How are we to cope with and overcome the vanity and pretense of nearly 16,000,000 political office holders? They presume powers bordering on magic, in the sense of "producing extraordinary results."

To repeat what I have written numerous times before: (1) ours is not a numbers problem; (2) it is not a selling but a learning problem.

- Every good movement in all history has been in response to an infinitesimal minority. One of many examples: The very few who did the thinking which resulted in The Declaration, Constitution and Bill of Rights.

- Ideas cannot be "sold"; neither can they be thrust into the minds of others. The correct formula? Become so excellent in explaining the freedom way of life that others will seek your tutorship. Become mentors! Excellence begets excellence whatever the endeavor—be it cooking, science, golf, music or whatever. All experience attests to this fact.

The achievement of these aspirations requires extraordinary effort, of a kind and quality which only those who love freedom are *happy* to expend. This is testimony to the fact that freedom is far from free.

It is interesting to observe what others have had to say on this important subject. Walter Weisenburger was President of the National Association of Manufacturers during the early forties, and one of the most brilliant freedom devotees any business organization ever had. He pointed out that: "American business needs fewer orders from the government and more orders from customers."

No one, from the local policeman to the President of the U.S.A., is aware of even a small fraction of the millions of orders from our 78,000 governmental units—national, state and local. But we do know that every order beyond keeping the peace and invoking a common justice makes creative effort more difficult and hinders a progress that would be far greater than now.

One example should suffice to make the point. Governmental

intervention makes for heavy taxation, deficits, and inflation. Individuals, then, are left with less money of their own to spend, but the interventionist government pressure causes prices to rise relentlessly—as in the case of automobiles and motor fuel. Prices of larger model automobiles, especially, are now so high that the supply exceeds the demand. Dealers' lots are filled with unsold cars, and one of our largest manufacturers is being bailed out with a government loan. What is needed, obviously, are more orders from customers; impossible unless there be fewer orders from government.

Wrote Will Durant: "Freedom is not inborn or imperishable. It must be acquired anew by every generation." We do not inherit an understanding of freedom—or the necessary devotion to it— from the previous generation. Freedom perishes unless acquired *anew* in one's own generation and by a number sufficient to constitute an *attracting* leadership! There are many steps to such a glorious achievement. What are they? Two of them are (1) new phrasing for old truths, and (2) the necessary disciplines required if we would be free.

- Such old-time phrasings as "the home of the brave and the land of the free" or "Liberty and Union, now and forever, one and inseparable" have long since been meaningless— mere empty sounds. So, in our time, we search for new ways to explain freedom, even though no one will ever be able to explain it fully. Try to explain Creation! It is impossible. Creative action at the human level borders on this difficulty. One way of phrasing will be apprehended by a few, another phrasing by a few others. Explaining liberty is, indeed, a task now and forever.

- What are the necessary disciplines? It is perpetual "training that develops self-control, character, efficiency." In our case, the basic discipline is the perpetual study of freedom that we may better understand and explain this wondrous way of life. To repeat a wise thought by G. K. Chesterton: "The world will never starve for want of wonders, but only for want of wonder." If we want freedom to continue working its wonders, we must allow for the mystery of creativity.

Finally, two wise thoughts, the first by Felix Morley: "If people do not possess the capacity to govern themselves, they are inevitably governed by others." This is an excellent and improved phrasing to describe our present politico-economic holocaust: "great or widespread destruction."

The second is by Edmund Burke who expressed the same idea two centuries earlier: "It is ordained in the eternal constitution of things, that men of intemperate minds cannot be free. Their passions forge their fetters." Those of intemperate minds—going to socialistic extremes—lack the capacity to govern themselves. The result? An unholy and tyrannical extreme: governed by governments!

The alternative? Self-government, self-reliance, self-responsibility, self-consciousness. Easy? No! But only those who move in the direction of these intellectual, moral and spiritual goals—while happy in their pursuit—gain a profound awareness: *Freedom is far from free!*

3

PRE-EMPTION: LEGAL THIEVERY

Petty thievery is punished, but thievery on a grand scale is honored by a triumphal procession. **—SENECA**

Of all the devilish tactics which are leading the U.S.A. head-on into socialism *pre-emption* tops the list. Lamentably, the word is not in most people's vocabulary, and try to find even a freedom devotee who is aware of its causal effects. All of us have some homework to do if we are to realize that pre-emption is legal thievery on the grand scale!

Before going further, it is necessary to define the *proper role* of government. One cannot tell what government should or should not do unless one knows what government is and is not.

Government is organized force! It issues edicts backed by a constabulary—a physical force which can be symbolized by the clenched fist. Find out what the fist can and cannot do and we will know what government should and should not do. The fist can restrain, inhibit and penalize. What, in all good conscience, should be restrained, inhibited and penalized? The answer was given in the moral codes long before Christianity: the "Thou shalt nots"—destructive actions such as stealing, killing, and so on. Inhibit those destructive acts: that's what government can legitimately do—period!

Most important is the answer to what government can *not* do. It is not and can never be a *creative* force. All such forces are spiritual in the sense that discoveries, inventions, insights, ideas, intuitive flashes are spiritual. Everything by which we live and prosper shows forth in the spiritual before it is manifested in the material. A water glass is inconceivable had not some cave dweller discovered how to harness fire. A jet plane would be impossible had not some Hindu ten centuries ago invented the concept of zero. All modern chemistry and physics would be impossible had we to rely on Roman numerals.

What, then, is government's proper role? It is to inhibit all destructive actions, keep the peace, and invoke a common justice. Leave all creative actions—education or whatever—to citizens acting privately, voluntarily, competitively, cooperatively. That's how to draw the line.

The dictionary's definition of pre-emption is: "To seize before anyone else can; *excluding others*." Let's pose a hypothetical example. Government has not pre-empted welfare. We can, if we so choose, give to others as generously as we please. However, government spends so much on welfare—billions of dollars annually—that most citizens behave as if it were pre-empted. Their reaction to a starving neighbor: "That's the government's job." Were they not afflicted with the pre-emptive error, they would share their last loaf of bread with their starving neighbor—the practice of Judeo-Christian charity.

What do I mean by legal pre-emption? I am speaking of any productive, peaceful activity or service which government puts out of bounds to ordinary citizens, like the service of delivering private messages as a profit-making enterprise. The national government has legally pre-empted this service; it runs the U.S. Postal Service, and there is a law on the books making it a crime for any private citizen to go into the business of first-class mail delivery. There are cases in the courts periodically, prosecuting some entrepreneur who sought to set up a business for the peaceful service of carrying private messages for profit.

Legal pre-emption of any peaceful service—the Post Office is only one of thousands of instances—results in a species of thievery. In the case of mail delivery, legal pre-emption *robs* entrepreneurs—thousands of them around the nation of the opportunity to deliver mail. Were this opportunity thrown open to anyone, many would regard mail delivery as the most favorable occupational choice available to them. Why should they be forbidden to make this choice?

Mail delivery is as much a creative activity as voice delivery. Prior to 1864 the voice could be delivered about 50 yards. Left to the free market where the wisdom is, the miracle: the human voice can be delivered around the world at the speed of light— one-seventh of a second! One of many personal experiences: I once phoned my office from Switzerland, and it took no longer than phoning a next-door neighbor. This is an example of the efficiency of the market.

Contrast the situation in Argentina, where the phone system is "run" by government. Recently, I tried to call my office from Buenos Aires. I waited several hours. Why? Pre-emption by a political collective—the government—from which creative wisdom never has, does not, and never will originate.

Governmental pre-emption of mail delivery results in ever-increasing prices and the service declines year by year. Leave mail delivery to the market and the result would be no less phenomenal than present-day voice delivery by the market! No one in today's world can imagine how wondrous it would be any more than Leonardo da Vinci could have foreseen the wonders of a 747 Jet!

It is my belief that creative wisdom never originates in political action. Why doesn't it? Why is political action so devoid of rationality, discernment, sagacity? The correct answer to this difficult-to-solve *riddle* would open up a politico-economic gold mine: freedom!

Presumably, our 16,000,000 officeholders—federal, state and local—are equal in intelligence to those who elect them. Why, then, are their speeches and writings so often lacking in creative wisdom?

Here is a suggested answer: An officeholder tends to speak or to write as a member of a party or as the voice of a political collective. The individual and the personal are unwanted by-products when words are fed into the political meatgrinder, only to come out as a homogenized communique! The truth is ultimately a personal witness issuing from a man's highest self; written or spoken words reflect the mind and heart of the person who utters them and stands by them. His very being vouches for them; they are from the soul and make their just impact on the soul of another. Perhaps Emerson was getting at this point when he said, "What you *are* speaks so loud that I cannot hear what you say!" Words, to have weight, must match the man who voices them; take away the man and his words have lost any attachment to reality.

And it is precisely this we are guilty of when we operate as a committee. The mere spokesman for a committee, a sect, a party, or any other kind of collective, is issuing words that are anchored to no reality. They are adrift! A manifesto issued by a collective is but one set of words loosely related to another set of words; the personal note is eliminated, and with it the truth.

True, there are a growing number of officeholders who are statesmen and speak for freedom as individuals—separate and apart from the political collective. Also, there have been office-holders who have stepped aside from their political role and have prospered as creative citizens efficiently serving consumers.

The freedom way of life has its birth in a nation of self-respon-sible, self-reliant citizens—individualism—but *never* from a col-lectivistic society as Russia. *Political collectives do not nor can they create!*

In the foregoing I have commented on government pre-emp-tion of mail delivery, and the disastrous consequences that have ensued. Contrast this with the field of voice delivery, where the market is free and miracles are commonplace. The Postal Service is not the only instance of political pre-emption; there are thou-sands of others. Many persons will thoughtlessly assume that some of these other thousands of pre-emptions are okay. But, if the same reasoning be applied to any instance of pre-emption as has been used in the cases of mail and voice delivery, the answer will be an emphatic, "NO!"

Let us not cast the derogatory eye only at political officehold-ers. Many citizens in all walks of life seek private advantage from some form of pre-emptive action. Labor unions keep non-members and youngsters from job opportunities; minimum wage laws outlaw the more or less unskilled.

Then there are businessmen who obtain or advocate embargoes or tariffs in their effort to pre-empt freedom to trade goods and services. There is not an occupational category in which pre-emptive thinking or action does not exist—more or less. Thus, we have "thievery on the grand scale, honored by a triumphal procession."

The nearest one can come to remedying this thievery is by example: *Make oneself an honest person and there will be one less rascal in the world!*

4

GOOD INTENTIONS GONE ASTRAY

The road to hell is paved with good intentions.
                    —RICHARD BAXTER

This English Divine (1615–91) provides an excellent phrasing for my thesis: Disaster results from certain policies however well-meaning the people may be who sponsor them. We are on a hellish road, although it may be conceded that the intentions of our countless "pavers" are good—in their own view. They are afflicted with a shortsightedness that has only one remedy: a better understanding of why their notions are against everyone's interest, including their own.

All of us who believe in freedom should try to surpass each other in putting brighter and brighter lights along life's pavement. It is not enough that one's intentions be good. People with good intention, but whose ideas are afflicted with fallacies, cannot avoid acting against their own interests, as well as everyone else's. Here are a few thoughts on the hellish results.

Tariffs are anti-consumer. One of several flaws in early American history was a tariff law. There were two excuses: (1) revenue, which was skimpy and (2) protection of our infant industries against the competition of European giants. Here are three questions and three answers:

1. What nation in all the world and in all history has had the most infant industrial starts? The U.S.A.
2. In what nation has there been the greatest number of infant industries growing into industrial giants? In the U.S.A.
3. In what nation has little-to-bigness development faced the greatest competition? In the U.S.A. where there have been and are now more industrial giants than have existed elsewhere.

A friend of mine became one of the wealthiest men in America by discovering novel ways to lower his costs several years before his competitors. By the time they had caught up with him, he had devised new ways.

Much to my surprise, he one day advocated tariffs. Why? To outlaw foreign competitors who had found ways to undersell him. Today, there are thousands of leading businessmen who advocate tariffs and embargoes to destroy competition. The extent to which free trade is squelched, locally or internationally, to that extent are consumers deprived of goods and services.

Labor unions are anti-employee. As every employer should be free to hire or fire whomever he pleases, so should every individual be free to choose his employment. Such freedom does not exist in any business, educational institution, or any other endeavor dominated by unions. The labor union leaders, by rea-

son of coercive force, granted by government, become employ-
ers, deciding who shall have work and who shall not. Walter
Reuther, head of the United Auto Workers for years, truly believed in his domineering role: "*Only a moron* would believe
that the millions of private economic decisions being made inde-
pendently of each other will somehow harmonize in the end [free-
dom] and bring us out where we want to be."[1]

Today, there are some 20,000,000 members of labor unions,
about one-fifth of the adult population. Reflect on how this limits
the right of access to job opportunities by nonunion citizens.
Briefly, coercion is used to prevent nonunion people from working in unionized endeavors; force is used to prevent willing workers from taking jobs which union members have vacated, whether
by reason of old age or death or whatever.

If we concede that such mental delinquency is opposed to life's
high purpose—an improving righteousness—then all the Reuth-
ers and all citizens would fare far better were there no coercive
labor unions!

Government handouts are anti-charity. Judeo-Christian charity
in its highest form is anonymous—giving aid to those in distress
without disclosing the identity of the giver.[2] Not only keep one's
benevolence unknown to the recipient, but even to one's self.
Forget it! Let nothing enter the mind which leads to such an
assessment of self as "What a great Samaritan am I!" Such is to
destroy one of the greatest of all virtues: humility!

According to the above characteristic of true charity, government handouts are the very opposite. Instead of secrecy there is

---

[1]See the *New York Times*, June 30, 1962.
[2]For an instructive and inspirational book on this subject see, *Magnificent Ob-
session*, a novel by Lloyd Douglas (Boston: Houghton Mifflin Company, 1938).

blatancy: "to bellow; disagreeably loud; noisy . . . *obtrusive*." The "giver" government is not the source of its handouts; rather, government merely redistributes the livelihood of all citizens. If this be charity, then charity is evil, a sin of the first order!

One more comment about government handouts. Whenever government pre-empts any activity, citizens forget how personally to practice it. As it is today, when a neighbor is in need the common reaction is to regard caring for the needy as government's role. But were there no pre-emption, we would share our last loaf of bread with our neighbors in distress. Government handouts are, indeed, anti-charity!

Price controls are anti-trade. Assume there were no trade, that you were compelled to live on what you now produce or know how to produce. You would perish! Trading—exchanging our specializations—is implicit in survival. This is self-evident.

We Americans have literally millions of specializations. The freer the results of specialization are to flow and configurate, the more will prosperity grace our lives; the less free, the worse off we are. There are countless obstacles to the free flowing of goods and services, and prosperity is one of them! "We have it made," as many "think," and thus their talents lie dormant—thinking deadened! Eternal vigilance is the price of liberty, and prosperity may cause us to forget—an all too human frailty.

There is, however, another "frailty" of which we should beware: the persistent faith in price controls. Anyone may rewrite the price tag, but the real price of a good cannot be controlled by law. Price controls tell lies!

Observe the people who say they are for freedom yet insist on price controls—the same as saying they favor *people control!* The fruits of your labor are *yours* no less than your existence is yours. It follows that the prices you can obtain for your goods and services in willing exchange are as much yours as your life. For government to control your prices is to control your life. Wrote Edmund Burke: "No government ought to exist for the purpose of checking the prosperity of its people or allow such a principle in its policy." Prices are no more government's business than deciding how long we should live.

Child labor laws are anti-youth. Wrote the American Bishop, Edmund Janes (1807–76): "The interests of childhood and youth are the interests of mankind." If we are to have a society graced with citizens devoted to freedom we must see to it that our children are not dominated by authoritarians. Are they now? Yes, in several ways. Child labor laws, for example. Young people are not free to accept employment until the age of 16! Work opportunities that make for growth and help them learn the problems of adulthood are denied. Result? Political domineering on the rampage!

The minimum wage today is $3.35 per hour, this being a government edict sponsored by labor unions. Why this immoral, destructive law? The minimum wage eliminates competition by youngsters in the labor market, thus giving a special privilege or advantage to labor unions. Stunting the growth of future citizens in this fashion may well be the most anti-freedom device ever devised!

When we assume that life's highest purpose is a growth in awareness, perception, consciousness—a correct and laudable assumption—we must perceive child labor laws as nothing less than a death sentence. Youth committed to an intellectual tomb! That I, at the age of 82, have been able to write this, my 27th book on the freedom thesis, is partially due to a childhood not thus encumbered. Work was part of my daily routine.

Was I a *laborer?* Yes, and not only in childhood but into my advanced adulthood. "Laborer" is a label I refuse to relinquish. From the age of eleven to eighteen—when I entered World War I—my work week was 102 hours. Up and away to work at four o'clock, cleaning stables, milking cows, six hours at school, evening chores on the farm, clerking in the village store until nine o'clock week days and until midnight on Saturdays. Cows were milked on Sundays, too! Work is still an everyday matter with me. If all of this doesn't qualify me as a laborer, pray tell, what does?

One summer there was a break in the above routine—working 60 hours a week running a cement mixer. The pay? *Five cents* an hour! That's quite a contrast to the present minimum wage of $3.35 an hour! Given a choice between my 5 cents with opportunities unlimited or the present death-sentence law, what would my answer be? I'll let my readers make the guess.

The above are mere samplings of good intentions gone astray. Today, there are more than one can count. Your and my role? See if we can improve the clarity of the explanations here offered. Have a try at explaining such ideological paradoxes as: Social Security is Anti-Security, Maximum Hours are Anti-Work, Energy Control is Anti-Energy, Medicare is Anti-Health, Rationing is Anti-Plenty—on and on!

A Latin scholar of more than 2,000 years ago gave to us a splendid idea: *Begin to be now what thou would be hereafter!*

5

WOE BETIDE YE OF LITTLE TRUST

The soul and spirit that animates and keeps up society is mutual trust. **—JOHN SOUTH**

The economist, Dr. Donald Kemmerer, calls our attention to a lamentable fact: "The rotting fabric of trust causes our buying power to melt away as a cube of ice in July."[1] While the dissolution may not be that fast, it is deplorably rapid. His metaphor helps to dramatize the cause and curse of inflation.

Wise men of the past have had a lot to say about "trust," and quite a few held views similar to the Englishman, Lord William Burleigh (1520–98): "Trust not any man with thy life, credit or estate." Why such a negative view about this important virtue? Burleigh lived in the age of mercantilism, a form of authoritarianism similar to our present planned economy and welfare state—little know-nothings afflicted with the I-Am-It syndrome. Trust them with one's pocketbook or way of life? Might as well leave one's fate to a Hitler!

---

[1] See "The Rotting Fabric of Trust," *The Freeman*, March 1980.

22

Admittedly, trust requires a great deal of discrimination. Never trust a thief or those who advocate political thievery, "from each according to his ability, to each according to his need"—plunderers! But reflect on the countless persons we can trust, and by trusting we increase adherence to this important virtue. Wrote Henry David Thoreau: "I think that we may safely trust a good deal more than we do. We may waive just so much care of ourselves as we honestly bestow elsewhere."

Imagine a person who never trusted anyone. His life would be filled with bitterness and error, resulting in despondency—a hopeless character. Trust falls in the reciprocal category; it furthers mutuality. The fewer persons I trust, the fewer will trust me; conversely, trust begets trust.

Reflect on the vast majority of the world's people—including ever so many in the U.S.A.—who do not trust the private ownership, free market, limited government way of life; there is little trust in the potentially miraculous results of citizens by the millions acting *creatively* as they please. What is the thrust of this general lack of trust? Toward socialism! Citizens vote and install in public office those who know no more or even less than they do, giving politicians power to run our lives. An utterly fallacious trust! Ergo, the thrust is toward the Command Society—freedom to produce and exchange goods and services made increasingly difficult, inflation and rising prices. Difficulties compounded!

Thoreau was right: "We may *safely* trust a great deal more than we do." Safely and also wisely, for those of us who trust others assuredly make fewer mistakes than those who are bogged down in distrust. In order to minimize our own mistakes—errors—we must learn from others—past and present. And we can learn from even the most unlikely sources. Wrote John Maynard Keynes: "By a continuing process of inflation, governments can confiscate, secretly and unobserved, an important part of the wealth of their citizens."[2]

For freedom's sake, let us look for light from whatever source. Psalms 8:2: "Out of the mouths of babes and sucklings has thou ordained strength." Doubtless, the brightest light is to be found among those whose aim is the same as that of Cardinal John Henry Newman: "Lead, Kindly Light, amid the encircling gloom, Lead Thou me on!"

Trust is defined as the "firm belief or confidence in the honesty, integrity, reliability, justice . . . of another person . . . faith, reliance."

There are millions of citizens who sincerely believe in the planned economy and the welfare state, but who can be trusted in ever so many other respects. Most of them can be trusted to keep their promises, pay their bills, obey the laws be they good or bad, do their best at their profession, be it cooking, carpentry, washing windows, operating machines or whatever. Trusting these people when and if trust is deserved is not only good for those of us who trust them but, sooner or later, may cause a few of them to abandon their socialism and put a trust in freedom!

What about the virtues bound up with "trust"—honesty, integrity, reliability, faith, justice? There are tens of thousands of men and women who labor for the world's many airlines, and they constitute one example, among many, that deserves reflection. These laborers range from those who keep the planes spic and span, to baggage loaders, to flight attendants, to engineers, to the Captains.

Having flown more than 2,000,000 miles during the last 62

---

[2]From *The Economic Consequences of the Peace* by John Maynard Keynes, 1920.

years, I have some familiarity with exemplars of the above-mentioned virtues.

- I have never encountered dishonesty in the personnel.
- As to integrity, broken promises are rarely encountered.
- Reliability? Name something more worthy of reliance. Air travel is by far the safest form of transportation. Millions of miles are flown daily in perfect safety.
- Do I then have an unwavering faith in air travel? Not quite. Why?
- Only in justice do they fail. All of these laborers, including the Captains—now and then an exception—are members of labor unions. They resort to coercion as a means of working fewer hours and getting higher pay. A Captain on a U.S.A. airline receives pay as high as $117,000 a year and the limit of labor is 75 hours per month. Coercion is sinful!

Longfellow gave good counsel to you and me and all who labor in this or that endeavor, including airline personnel:

> Man-like it is, to fall into sin;
> Fiend-like it is, to dwell therein;
> Christ-like it is, for sin to grieve;
> God-like it is, all sin to leave.

6

LITTLE MEN CAUSE BIG GOVERNMENT

The real difference between men is energy. A strong will, a settled purpose, an invincible determination, can accomplish almost anything; and in this lies the distinction between great men and little men. **—THOMAS FULLER**

The English divine, Thomas Fuller (1608–61), gives us an enlightening distinction between great and little men. There is no genius in life unless genius is buttressed by energy—an idea supported by the English dramatist and poet, Nicholas Rowe (1674–1718): "The wise and active conquer difficulties by daring to attempt them. Sloth and folly shiver and shrink at sight of toil and hazard, and make the impossibility they fear."

When little men cast long shadows, the sun is setting on a civilization. Little men now abound by the millions. They do, indeed, cast their shadows—shiver and shrink at the sight of toil and hazard. This accounts, in no small measure, for the growing socialism.

These little men, having no high purpose of their own, are attracted by political folderol—"mere nonsense." And their naivete, in turn, attracts modern medicine men, representing them-

26

selves as having supernatural powers: "Elect me to office and I'll handle all your problems."

We have about 16,000,000 individuals elected or appointed to political office—federal, state and local. With a few notable exceptions, what is their remedy for the *woes* of the little men? It is to promise something for nothing—taking from those who produce and giving to those who only consume. This is planned chaos, but both the little men and the political medicine men glory in this pandemonium—"the abode of demons . . . the capital of Hell!"

Conceded, both groups are presumed innocent of wrongdoing as they raise havoc with freedom. Their innocence sprouts from their naivete—"an almost foolish lack of worldly wisdom." Let's explore the remedy: a Heavenly Wisdom!

This wisdom is possessed by *great* men—men of energy! Wrote Goethe: "Energy will do anything that can be done in *this* world; and no talents, no circumstances, no opportunities will make a two-legged animal a man without it."

Not everything can be done in this world of ours. Some things are impossible; other things are difficult and can be accomplished only by the expenditure of much energy over a long period of time. Reflect on Cro-Magnon man of some 35,000 years ago. He made tools of flint and of bones, and left traces of his art in cave paintings. His brain was large, suggesting a mental potential and an untapped reservoir of energy that links him to modern man. But it took 35,000 years for the creature, Man, to transform the simple artifacts of Cro-Magnon man into the miraculous man-made environment of modern technology. Cro-Magnon man would have been flabbergasted had he been able to foresee the world in which you and I live; our mental powers and energies are much more fully invested in our creations than were his. This evolutionary advance occurred because in each generation from his day to ours some human beings made full use of the powers they possessed at the time, and drew the rest of us on. By the same token, we would be equally amazed if we could catch a glimpse of the world in the year 36,980!

The eminent psychologist, Fritz Kunkel, wrote: "*Immense hidden powers* lurk in the unconscious of the most common men, indeed, of all people without exception." What a boon to civilization were all individuals to recognize their hidden powers!

Recognition, however, is but the initial step. The idea is useless—lies dormant—unless accompanied by a dynamic and everflowing energy, the power of implementation!

Energy is necessary for high-grade behavior, but there are, as Fuller noted, several related virtues which must be practiced if men are to be great. Wrote Tryon Edwards: "The highest obedience in the spiritual life is to be able always, and in all things, to say, 'Not my will, but *thine* be done'."

The spiritual life ranges from the highest thoughts of the finite mind to Infinite Consciousness. When we make the latter life's guideline and adhere strictly to it—looking always to The Source—burdens will be light and our duties a joy.

Another required virtue: a settled purpose. Wrote the American clergyman, Theodore T. Munger (1830–1910): "There is no road to success but through a clear strong purpose. Nothing can take its place. A purpose underlies character, culture, position, attainment of every kind."

Reflect on the number of individuals who go through life with no purpose—as a ship without a rudder, going every which way. For these poor souls, life is no more than a meandering adventure; they wander aimlessly and idly.

The secret of success in life is to have a supreme purpose, one which harmonizes all other strivings. Individuals vary, so each person makes his choice of a lifelong goal from among the many alternatives open to him. Freedom prevails in a society when each person has maximum latitude for making these decisions. Life's purpose realized; what a reward!

Fuller's final virtue, if great men are to be among us, is "an invincible determination." Wrote the English critic and author, William Hazlitt (1784–1870): "There is nothing more to be esteemed than a manly firmness and decision of character. I like a person who knows his own mind and sticks to it; who sees at once what, in given circumstances, is to be done and then does it."

Here is what a few other great men have written on this subject:

Not education but character is man's greatest need and man's greatest safeguard.   —*Herbert Spencer*

The great hope of society is in individual character.
                                        —*W. E. Channing*

If you would create something you must be something.
                                                —*Goethe*

We cannot dream ourselves into great character, but must hammer and forge this virtue in our daily living.

I wrote in a previous paragraph about the *woes* of the little men. The longer they continue in that lamentable category, the more *woes* will they experience. As Shakespeare said:

> When one is past another care we have;
> Thus woe succeeds woe; as wave a wave.

The opposite of *woes* are *blessings,* a virtue of great men. The more they recognize and count their blessings, the more are they blest. *Let us appreciate our countless blessings.*

7

GOODNESS: THE FIRST STEP TO FREEDOM

None can love freedom heartily, but good men, the rest love not freedom, but license.
—JOHN MILTON

John Milton (1608–74), English poet and author of the renowned plea for freedom of the press, *Areopagitica,* referred to "good *men,*" presumably in the generic sense, meaning male and female. He stood steadfastly against the hierarchy that ruled in his time and may well have been the first outright exponent of the right to freely publish written material. This is a seminal freedom; implicit in such a position is freedom of speech, freedom of religion, freedom to act creatively, and to produce and exchange as anyone pleases. Briefly, Milton achieved a monumental politico-economic and ideological breakthrough!

A first century Roman writer had this to say: "Some are good, some are middling, the most are bad." These judgments are no more than three generalities relating to human beings. Actually, there are as many variations in virtues and vices as there are individuals, multiplied by their variations from one moment to

30

the next—billions times billions! All of us are forever changing. However, these three categories of behavior deserve reflection for improvement's sake. The definitions:

- GOOD: Morally sound or excellent; specifically virtuous, pious, kind.
- MIDDLING: Mediocre; betwixt and between.
- BAD: The wicked, the evil, the unrighteous, the reprobates.

There are countless ways to evaluate the wide range between good and bad but I shall adhere strictly to the greatest of all concepts within the range of man. It is the freedom to act creatively as anyone chooses—*Creation at the human level!* Briefly, ideas and ideals versus notions and nonsense.

As to the bad—the wicked, the reprobates—it's a safe guess that even thieves have had, on rare occasions, a civil thought or done a kindly deed to someone. They may be 99 per cent but not 100 per cent bad. But, even at their best, they are devilish and a curse to mankind. An excellent warning in I Peter 5:8: "Be self-controlled and alert. Your enemy the devil prowls around like a roaring lion looking for someone to devour." Our quotable John Milton wrote in his *Paradise Lost:* "The Adversary of God and Man, Satan." Avoid these human evils and their nonsense as thou wouldst shun a deadly plague!

Before commenting on the next category, a confession: While that Roman writer's grading of people stimulated some thinking, I believe he erred as to numbers. Here is my revised version: Very few are good, the vast majority are middling, and the bad number no more than one in many thousands.

The middling—the betwixt and between—wreak far more havoc on society than the bad. We know not all the reasons, but for one, there are so many more of them. Reflect on the infinite numbers of dubious "thoughts"—errors—that sprout from vast multitudes. Three thoughts by others on this point:

> The multitude *unawed* is insolent; once seized with fear, contemptible and vain.   —*David Mallet*

> License they mean when they cry liberty.   —*John Milton*

> The mass never comes up to the standard of its best member, but on the contrary degrades itself to the level of the lowest.
> —*Henry David Thoreau*

Unless an individual stands in awe of Creation's wonders, he thinks of his finite self as the only source of our countless blessings. The unawed are, indeed, vain.

Most of those among the betwixt and between will claim an adherence to liberty for no more reason than its favorable connotation. By labeling themselves friends of freedom, they feel less evil as they indulge in countless forms of license—"freedom to deviate from strict conduct, rule or practice; excessive, undisciplined freedom, *constituting an abuse of liberty.*"

Every pronouncement or action which impinges on the right of anyone to live creatively as he or she pleases—embargoes, tariffs, minimum wages, maximum hours, coercive taking from some and giving to others, government subsidies, on and on—is *pure license.*

Wrote the American clergyman, William Sprague (1795–1876): "In the same proportion that ignorance and vice [license] prevails in a republic, will the government partake in despotism." For proof, merely take a look at what's going on in America!

Reflect, finally, on good men *who love freedom heartily.* Here is an excellent thought from E. H. Chapin: "Goodness consists not in the outward things we do but in the inward thing we are. To be good is the great thing.'' I feel certain that this clergyman, in referring critically to ''the outward things,'' had in mind those who make a public display, those whose pomposity—''self-importance''—has to do with reforming others, that is, making others like themselves.

''The inward thing,'' by contrast, means improving the only individual within one's own dominion, namely, one's self! Result? To the extent one succeeds in self-improvement, to that extent will others seek his or her tutorship! This is the only solution to a reversal from our present socialism to a hoped-for freedom. *To be good is, indeed, the great thing!*

The number of people who adhere strictly to the principles of freedom is small—relative to the total population. But this tiny handful does far more good than most of us imagine.

The Sage of Concord passed on to posterity a correct methodology: ''Look not mournfully to the past—it comes not back again; wisely improve the present—it is thine; go forth to meet the shadowy future without fear, and with a manly heart.''

8

DEPENDENCE AND INDEPENDENCE

These two things, contradictory as they may seem, go together, manly dependence and manly independence, manly reliance and manly self-reliance.
—WILLIAM WORDSWORTH

What a wise observation by this English poet (1770–1850), who knew that dependence and independence are complementary, when people are free.

In a free society everyone enjoys the enormous benefits which flow from individual specialization and the ensuing voluntary exchanges of specialized goods and services. In a division of labor society every one of us relies on the work of others, and he relies on himself to acquire the marketable skills uniquely his own. Each person's market offering of goods and services is judged by his peers in terms of the value it has for them, according to each person's independent judgment. The impersonality of the market process makes for individual independence. No doubt this is the "manly independence" Wordsworth had in mind.

34

But there is also an unmanly dependence of the sort that assures "inferiority and corruption": a pretty good description of socialism.

Our Pilgrim Fathers experienced such debilitating dependence during the first three years after landing at Plymouth Rock in 1620! While they did not use the modern phrasing, they practiced the communal formula, "From each according to his ability, to each according to his need," and backed by force. No freedom of choice! Karl Marx gave the notion the current formulation 250 years later.

This unmanly type of dependence is otherwise known as robbing Peter to pay Paul—a procedure often associated with Robin Hood. Observe what the dictionary has to say about this lowbrow character:

> Robin Hood, in English legend, a traditional outlaw of the 12th century who lived with his followers in Sherwood Forest, and robbed the rich to help the poor; he is the hero of many ballads and tales, celebrated for his courage, gaiety, courtesy, skill as an archer, etc.

There was no real Robin Hood to rob the rich to help the poor, for this legendary figure never existed. Nevertheless, the fairy tale has persisted. So powerful has been this myth that it works its devastations upon all nations in today's world—no exception.

Those who embrace the myth are just as happy as those endowed with common sense! They get government to rob the rich "to help the poor" and, by so doing, grant themselves a sense of absolution. Examples abound by the millions, and few are the citizens who do not advocate this or that form of intervention. Hence today's world plague of unmanly dependence.

But let us turn back to our Pilgrim Fathers and their experience with communal life. Why did they abandon this nonsense? They were starving! Starvation or the threat thereof—like any other calamity, present or threatened—stimulates remedial thinking, now and then. In the winter of 1623 in Plymouth, Governor William Bradford met with the remaining Pilgrims, pointing out the fallacies of the ways that had led to their disaster, and presenting a truth that led to *Independence* in our country. Here is his wisdom, abbreviated:

> Our scheme, from each according to ability to each according to need, has not worked. To give presupposes something in the warehouse to give. Most of the time ours has been empty. Come springtime we shall try a new idea: to each according to merit or productivity. Each shall have what he or she produces!

Here we have the principle of private ownership—fundamental to the free society—expressed as simply and succinctly as any economist ever phrased it. Result? Following Bradford's advice, the rewards were to be dispensed in accord with productivity, so father, mother and children joined to till the fields! To each his own!

The colonists worked in freedom, with each entitled to enjoy the fruits of his or her own labor. Productivity increased, and the result was unprecedented abundance, widely shared. This new society of free and prosperous citizens constituted the real American revolution. It was unrelated to the fracas with King George III, the Revolutionary War. Rather, it was a revolutionary concept of a voluntary society of free people supplanting the ancient practice of communal living.

Throughout history mankind had been killing each other by the millions over the question of which form of authoritarianism should preside as sovereign over man. The argument had not been between freedom and authoritarianism; it had been a contest to decide which form of political gangsterism should rule.

The adoption of private property principles by the Pilgrims led to freedom as never before practiced and 150 years later culminated in the Declaration of Independence, the greatest political document ever written. The Declaration unseated government as the endower of men's rights and *placed the Creator there!*

Independence—with its complement of *manly* dependence—prevailed throughout the nineteenth century. Why this success, never before achieved in all history? Because *manly* citizens were not plundering one another or turning to government for handouts. Where, then, did Americans look for their welfare? Only to self, resulting in a *manly self-reliance!*

Henry Ward Beecher observed that, "Success is full of promise till men get it, and then it is as a last year's nest, from which the bird has flown." During much of the twentieth century in the United States, the flight has been from the nest of *manly virtues*—a flight toward socialism!

Will Americans return to the nest? It depends on whether or not there is a return to the thinking and devoted practice that originally brought Independence to America:

- The revolutionary concept of private ownership initiated by our Pilgrim Fathers which led eventually to the Declaration of Independence.
- The belief that the Creator, not government, is the Endower of our right to life and livelihood.
- A return to *manly self-interest*.
- A manly respect for others, a mutual dependence. Being the most highly specialized people that ever existed, we have become *interdependent*. No one of us can go it alone. We are *absolutely* dependent on the free, uninhibited exchange

of our millions of varying bits of expertise. No government official—from the village mayor to the President of the U.S.A.—can any more properly direct what we shall produce or with whom we should exchange than I can take the Creator's place!

Let each of us know these Truths revealed by our Forefathers. To be found in John 8:32 is the blessing, the reward: *The truth shall make you free!*

9

THE FREE MIND

I call that mind free which protects itself against the usurpations of society, which does not cower to human opinion, which feels itself accountable to a higher tribunal than man's.
—WILLIAM ELLERY CHANNING

Channing gave us a formula which, if we understood and followed, would help restore our waning freedom. Our present growing socialism, communism—call the command society what you will—leads relentlessly toward *societal disaster*. Thus, it is important that we give his excellent thoughts some serious reflection.

Much of what follows are paraphrasings of ideas on the subject by outstanding scholars over the ages. As the French essayist, Montaigne, wrote, "I quote others better to express myself."

Mind unemployed is mind unenjoyed. Constant employment leads to ever higher activities of the mind; but mental inactivity—unemployment—accounts for mass behavior, serfdom, depressed spirits, and the like. Such people are in this sense mindless nonentities!

Possessing finite minds means that we can never grasp the infinitude of truth; but we do have the capacity to go forward from light to light. To grasp the infinitude of truth in the Cosmos, one would have to be as wise as the Creator—Infinite Consciousness, God! Perish such an absurd thought. Let each of us take our little steps, contributing our bits of light amidst the darkness. There is not enough darkness in the whole world to put out the light of one wee candle!

May every one of us without exception—socialists and anarchists, as well as freedom devotees—be free to speak our minds. The English poet, John Milton (1603–74), gave this aspect of freedom an excellent phrasing: "Give me the liberty to know, to think, to believe, and to *utter freely,* according to conscience, above all other liberties."

Suppose that you and I were to advocate the curbing of socialism (*planned* chaos) and of anarchy (*unplanned* chaos) by an anti-freedom method: attempting to silence believers. To employ this tactic would invite them to try silencing us—in a contest for power. Freedom would be lost. What then? Encourage our ideological opponents freely to express their views. Why? Such leniency on our part would be an attracting exemplarity. This increases the possibility of drawing a few of them to liberty.

Nothing is at last sacred but the integrity of our minds. Integrity is rarely mentioned or included among the virtues. The so-called cardinal virtues, as advanced in theology, are prudence, justice, fortitude, temperance. Integrity is omitted. I found, upon checking the largest of all quotation books, that integrity does not appear among the more than 1,000 headings. Indeed, so neglected is this virtue that one is tempted to side with Bernard Dougall: "Integrity was a word he couldn't even spell, let alone define." Such is the general unawareness of its meaning and importance!

When it comes to listing the virtues, I know only those that are important to me. Integrity is by all means first and foremost. For the others—charity, intelligence, justice, love and humility—I have no precise ranking. To me they are tied for second place.

It may be helpful to draw the distinction between integrity and wisdom, for my definitions so closely parallel each other.

- Integrity is an accurate reflection in word and deed of whatever one's highest conscience dictates as right.
- Wisdom is whatever one's highest conscience dictates as truth.

Conceded, one's highest conscience may not in fact be right but it is as close to righteousness as one can get. Also, one's highest conscience may not attain truth, but it as nearly approximates wisdom as is within one's reach. Fallibility applies in either case!

Who among us is truly educable in the higher realms of thought? Only persons of integrity! Those who pay no heed to conscience are forever the victims of expediency; they are governed by fickle opinions, pressures, mass sentiments, a desire for momentary acclaim. Wisdom—whatever one's highest conscience perceives as truth—is out of range simply because integrity—whatever one's highest conscience dictates as right—is not observed.

As if the above were not reason enough to strive for integrity! However, by far the most important reason remains: its *sacredness*. Though new to me, I now discover that this idea was perceived nearly 2,000 years ago: "The light of the body is the eye: if therefore thine eye be single, thy whole body shall be full of light." (Matthew 6:22)

What is the "light of the body"? It is truth, wisdom, enlightenment. The "eye" is perception. And what is the meaning of "if thine eye be single"? Refer to Webster for the definition of "single" as here used: "Not deceitful or artful, simple, honest, sincere." Shakespeare used the word in this same sense: "I speak with a *single* heart."

Single, in this sense, is directly linked with *integer,* meaning "Whole, entire, not divided." Contrasted to *single* is *double* which has the same original root as the word "duplicity." Such phrases as "double dealing," and "double talk" convey this connotation. *Integrity* is related to *integer;* and *single,* as used here, refers to *integrity.*

Phrased in modern idiom, Matthew's insight would read as follows: Enlightenment of the intellect and spirit of man depends on his powers of perception. If these powers be free from duplicity, that is, if they be grounded in pure integrity, man will be as much graced with enlightenment—wisdom—as is within his capacity.

Whatever the mysterious Universal Power—the radiant energy that flows through all life—it is blocked, cut off, stifled by duplicity in any of its forms. Expediency, lying, double talk, and the like are ferments of the soul through which Universal Power does not and cannot flow. "A double minded man is unstable in all his ways."—James 1:8

Only in integrity—when "the eye be single"—does the power of perception grow, evolve, emerge, hatch. The "whole body shall be full of light." Then, and only then, are such virtues as charity, intelligence, justice, love, humility within our reach.

This, however, poses a serious question: When are we warranted in becoming revolutionaries, resisting the present system of laws by passive and/or active disobedience?

There is no one—even among the revolutionaries—whose distaste for the plethora of oppressive laws on the statute books is greater than mine. The remedy, however, is to repeal these laws, not break them.

It takes no intelligence whatsoever to break the law; anyone can do that. But the repeal of oppressive laws calls for all the wit, skill, and genius man can muster.

Lawbreaking merely adds to the existing confusion. Repeal of oppressive laws, on the one hand, calls for a new and enlightened consensus. If an idea or action does not lead to enlightenment, it is worthless, if not downright destructive. When will I become a revolutionary? Not until the time when I am forbidden to freely write and speak the freedom thesis!

This is my answer—and challenge—to inquiring students. And I sign it not "Your obedient servant" or "Long live the King," but "Respectfully yours."

Finally, if we believe that we should do unto others that which we would not have them do unto us—a concern for others as well as self—we have one more among all the compelling reasons why we should strive first and foremost for integrity. Shakespeare put it well:

> . . . to thine own self be true,
> And it must follow, as the night the day,
> Thou canst not then be false to any man.

How avoid falsehood? Let us direct our minds to a practice of this Biblical Truth and Promise: "But whosoever looketh into *the* perfect law of Liberty, and continueth therein, he *being* not a forgetful hearer, but a doer of the work, this man shall be *Blessed* in his deed." (James 1:25)

10

LOVE MAKES THE WORLD GO ROUND

If the tender, profound and sym-phathizing love, practiced and recommended by Jesus, were paramount in every heart, the loftiest and most glorious idea of human society would be realized, and little be wanting to make this world a kingdom of heaven.
—FREDERICH KRUMMACHER

The title of this essay is a phrase taken from the work of the English novelist, Charles Dickens (1812–70). Krummacher, author of the quote, was a German theologian (1796–1868).

The Oxford Dictionary employs about 11,000 words to explain the meaning and nuances of "love." For instance, there are individuals who "love" to steal, "love" to run the lives of others, "love" to ridicule devotees of freedom, "love" applause, on and on.

Let me offer a definition from a personal experience, not included in the 11,000 words of the Oxford. My host at a seminar dinner remarked, "Since meeting you I have a new set of friends." He had until recently, he said, been consorting with "the fast set." Now that he had become interested in the freedom philosophy, he had new friends also interested in ideas on liberty. Impressive!

On retiring, it occurred to me that there was a relationship between "a new set of friends" and "the law of love," the Tolstoyan topic of our discussion. Searching for an answer, I fell asleep.

The next morning this question popped into mind: Who are *my* friends? A careful inventory revealed them to be those individuals, past and present, who were giving me light or the few who might be getting an idea or two from me; in brief, those in one's enlightenment circuit.

Moments later two ancient axioms came to mind: "God is love" and "God is light." Ergo, *love is light*—or enlightenment.

It is this kind of love that "makes the world go round"—the kind that lights the way to freedom.

We mortals have in Jesus the Perfect Exemplar. Many people think of the Second Coming as the reappearance of Christ. Such a belief requires nothing of you or me or anyone, except patience. In my judgment, there is a more immediately relevant interpretation. What, then, might be the deeper meaning? It is to see how nearly each of us can, in this life, approximate His Perfection! Seen in this light, Jesus is a Holy Magnetic Force, drawing individuals to love in its highest sense.

The thought above expressed is given support by the English author, David H. Lawrence, (1885–1930): "Love is a thing to be *learned*. It is a difficult, complex maintenance of individual integrity throughout the incalculable processes of interhuman polarity."

Assuredly, integrity is the number one virtue—thinking and acting in accord with one's highest idea of righteousness—the active love of truth. As Lawrence wrote, this is, indeed, a *learning* process!

Benjamin Franklin had an excellent thought as related to learning: "The man who does things makes many mistakes, but he never makes the biggest mistake of all—doing nothing."

The greatest thinkers of all time have erred on countless occasions. They acknowledge their mistakes but have learned that their errors open the intellectual doors to truth.

Doing nothing—no inclination to learn—is, indeed, the greatest mistake of all. The millions so afflicted, unconscious of their stalemated status, assess themselves as infallible. How does this lopsided assessment of self wreak its damage on freedom? They—a vast majority—elect "infallibles"—know-it-alls—to public office!

Wrote Goethe: "We are shaped and fashioned by what we love." Flowers grow better in the homes of those who love them. Animals—dogs, cats, birds or whatever—have an affection for those who love them. I have a love for highly-evolved individuals, past and present. It is easy to observe the effect of love on one's contemporaries, but rarely grasped is the possibility of a similar reaction by those who have passed to their reward a thousand or more years ago. Why this view?

Believing, as I do, in the immortality of the human spirit—consciousness—I am convinced that those of the past are as much aware of my feelings toward them as does my next-door neighbor know how I feel about him.

However, forget the effect of love for others. Merely keep in mind its benefit to self for "We are shaped and fashioned by what we love"—a Heavenly Blessing!

Wrote the German theologian, Frederick Spanheim (1809–59): "They are the true disciples of Christ, not who know the most, but who love the most." In other words, it is not knowing the most but doing the best that really counts. There are knowledgeable individuals who label themselves "atheists," but who are only reacting against some inadequate idea of *theos*. A genuine atheist would have to deny that there is anything in the Cosmos beyond his tiny mind. For him, there is no Creation; he is the Creator!

If love, "as recommended by Jesus, were paramount in every heart, the loftiest and most glorious idea of human society would be realized." It would, indeed, be "a kingdom on earth"!

The reality? Love is far from being paramount in every heart. Only a small fraction of any population is so graced, and this doubtless remains a distressing fact. The role of those who love?

First, it is to recognize that this is not a numbers problem. Jesus had only twelve disciples, including Judas, a betrayer.

Let each of us try, as best he can, to approximate the Perfection of Jesus. By such an effort we will enlarge the fraction of those who love. It is ordained in the Cosmic Design that: *Love makes the world go round!*

11

THE PRACTICE OF MANNERS AND MORALS

*Good manners are a part of good
morals; and it is as much our duty
as our interest to practice both.*
—JOHN HUNTER

One never knows whence bits of wisdom will appear. Hunter
was an English surgeon and wrote the above nearly two centuries
ago—an enlightening thought.

A few years later the American educator, Horace Mann, wrote:
"Manners easily and rapidly mature into morals." Manners—
"distinguished behavior," and morals—"right in conduct or
character," are twin virtues. Whoever combines good manners
with moral conduct possesses a virtuous magnetism that attracts
others to the freedom way of life. Here are a few reflections on
the practice of these virtues.

We are told in Romans 6:23 that "The wages of sin is death."
Assuredly, this has no reference to physical death but, rather, to
intellectual and spiritual demise. Among mankind's countless
sins are bad manners, and bad manners are deadly to good mor-

als! This accusation applies across the board, to freedom devotees no less than to socialists—a common and unholy trait! Bad manners are the mark of continuing adolescence—a sign of immaturity.

Socialists are those who resort to coercion to get their way in running the lives of others—be they politicians, labor union leaders, businessmen or whoever. Such people often speak and write despicably of those of us who stand for liberty: the right of one and all to act creatively as each pleases.

But what about freedom devotees? With few exceptions, we fall into that identical name-calling category—"the ignorant so-and-sos." This behavior not only hardens our opponents in their fallacious ways but it diminishes us for righteous ways. The extent to which we damn others to that extent reduces our capacity to *think* creatively. Tolerance is never easy, but we should not even think of our opponents derogatorily. The consequence of such thinking? Arrested adulthood!

Wrote the English mathematician and philosopher, Bertrand Russell (1872–1970): "Rules of conduct, whatever they be, are not sufficient to produce good results unless the ends sought are good."

Wise men, before beginning any action, look carefully at the end they have in mind. Wrote Emerson, "There is no end in nature, but every end is a beginning." "End" has two meanings: (1) an objective and (2) a conclusion. Emerson's reference was to the latter. Those of us whose objective—end—is freedom should realize that every step upward is but a beginning in more and better thinking—now and forever!

Wrote the Scottish divine, Hugh Blair (1728–1800): "Nothing, except what flows from the heart, can render even external manners truly pleasing." The "heart," as here used, means:

"inmost thoughts and feelings; consciousness; as I know in my *heart.*"

Unfortunately, most external manners are not from the heart; rather, they are mannerisms motivated by shallow desires—popularity, be-like-me-ness, and so on.

The ways of the heart, like Divine Omniscience, are mysterious. A stout heart is far more valuable than any material possession, and as Dickens wrote, "A loving heart is the truest wisdom." Why? It means an enduring love of such virtues as integrity and humility. Individuals so blest have manners pleasing to everyone who is capable of forming sensible judgments on human behavior.

Paraphrasing the Irish satirist and Dean of Saint Patrick's, Jonathan Swift (1667–1745): "Experience of the world enables some people to acquire a superficial polish and sophistry; but no one will have good manners whose nature is compounded of pride and incivility and who lacks common sense."

Millions of people acquire a superficial polish, a veneer of culture lacking substance. It has always been thus and doubtless will continue to be. Why this mass departure from common sense? It is an all-too-common addiction to sophistry: "unsound or misleading but *clever, plausible.*"

The American theologian, Nathaniel Emmons (1765–1840), came to our aid with this excellent analytical thought: "To reason justly from a false premise is the perfection of sophistry, which is more difficult to expose than to refute false reasoning."

Reasoning from a false premise can result only in countless errors. A striking example: Prior to Copernicus and Galileo—about four centuries ago—the common belief was that the sun revolves around the earth. Reflect on the deadly blow to progress in astronomy had that false premise not been corrected. A sound premise is essential in all fields, even more vital to freedom than to astronomy. Had Copernicus and Galileo not been *free* to un-scramble the traditional error in their field and in their time, we would still be blind to an important truth.

To those of us who would advance the freedom way of life, *consistency* is an absolute necessity; no leaks, no "buts"—never an approval of a single socialistic item. To be consistent with truth requires that one does his or her reasoning logically and deductively from a sound premise. Realizing this about thirty years ago, I sought a premise on which we at FEE might base our reasoning. I did one thing right; I went deep! If one's premise is founded on shallow or peripheral matters, consistency and truth are out of the question. So I asked the most difficult ques-tion I could think of, namely, what is man's earthly purpose? I could find no answer without bumping head on into three of my fundamental assumptions. They are as follows:

1. Man did not create himself, for it is easily demonstrable that man knows next to nothing about himself. So my first as-sumption is the primacy and supremacy of what I refer to as an Infinite Consciousness.
2. While it is difficult, it is nonetheless possible for the individ-ual to increase his own awareness, his own perception, his own consciousness.
3. I cannot demonstrate my third assumption but only know it to be a truth, namely, the immortality of the human spirit, this earthly moment being only the beginning.

With these assumptions in mind, what is man's earthly pur-pose? It is growth, development, emergence, evolution, hatch-ing. The Greek philosopher, Heraclitus, remarked, "Man is on earth as in an egg." This inspired C. S. Lewis to comment, "Man cannot go on being a good egg forever; he must hatch or rot.'' To hatch is to emerge, to evolve—man's earthly purpose. If we can reason logically and deductively from such a premise, our positions will be consistently sound. Here are two guidelines to determine whether or not one's premise is a good one:

1. If the individual cannot stand before God and man alike and pronounce his premise proudly, take another look at it.
2. If your premise does not require individual liberty, find one that does.

True, good manners lead to good morals. When enough individuals thus blest reason justly from a sound premise, *Liberty will again prevail!*

12

WHY THE PRESIDENT SAID NO

Though the people support the government, the government should not support the people.
—GROVER CLEVELAND

Grover Cleveland, while serving two terms as President, vetoed, I suspect, more interventionist or anti-freedom bills than any other President before or after his time. He understood the *limited* role of government and had the courage to stand by his convictions, a rare quality well exemplified in this veto message of February 16, 1887:

"I return without my approval House Bill No. 10203, entitled 'An act to enable the Commissioner of Agriculture to make a special distribution of seeds in the drought-stricken counties of Texas, and making an appropriation [of $10,000] therefor.'

"It is represented that a long-continued and extensive drought has existed in certain portions of the State of Texas, resulting in a failure of crops and consequent distress and destitution.

"Though there has been some difference in statements concerning the extent of the people's needs in the localities thus affected, there seems to be no doubt that there has existed a condition calling for relief; and I am willing to believe that, notwithstanding the aid already furnished, a donation of seed grain to the farmers located in this region, to enable them to put in new crops, would serve to avert a continuance or return of an unfortunate blight.

"And yet I feel obliged to withhold my approval of the plan, as proposed by this bill, to indulge a benevolent and charitable sentiment through the appropriation of public funds for that purpose.

"I can find no warrant for such an appropriation in the Constitution, and I do not believe that the power and duty of the General Government ought to be extended to the relief of individual suffering which is in no manner properly related to the public service or benefit. A prevalent tendency to disregard the limited mission of this power and duty should, I think, be steadfastly resisted, to the end that the lesson should be constantly enforced that though the people support the Government the Government should not support the people.

"The friendliness and charity of our countrymen can always be relied upon to relieve their fellow-citizens in misfortune. This has been repeatedly and quite lately demonstrated. Federal aid in such cases encourages the expectation of paternal care on the part of the Government and weakens the sturdiness of our national character, while it prevents the indulgence among our people of that kindly sentiment and conduct which strengthens the bonds of a common brotherhood."

All of the above as related to a mere pittance—$10,000. Today, politicians approve hundreds of billions for ever so many "salvations," and for no more reason than political popularity—a means of staying in office.

Our Founding Fathers, while more oriented toward the freedom way of life than any other group in all history, were not perfect. They were guilty of several errors, the most devastating being their acceptance of slavery. Presumably, they had a "reason": they wanted to bring the Southern States into the Union.

When the Negroes were finally freed, nearly all Americans believed slavery to be an evil in the past tense. But slavery assumed a new guise—in the form of subsidies and controls. "It is hardly lack of due process for the government to regulate that which it subsidizes," declared the U. S. Supreme Court in *Wickard vs. Filburn* (1942).

"He who pays the fiddler calls the tune." This certainly applies to the relationship between government and the citizens. When government subsidizes—pays—it regulates; it calls the tune which determines the extent of our enslavement.

Is "enslavement" too harsh a term? In 1884, that great British thinker, Herbert Spencer, wrote an unusual but thoughtful and realistic definition of slavery: "That which fundamentally distinguishes the slave is that he labours under *coercion* to satisfy another's desires. . . . What leads us to qualify our conception of slavery as more or less severe? Evidently the greater or smaller the extent to which effort is *compulsorily* expended for the benefit of another instead of for self-benefit."

Based on the authority of the Supreme Court, and deductive reasoning as well, it should be obvious that all who ask for subsidies are inviting regulations that diminish self-benefits. Such persons are asking for slavery—no less!

The same can be said of those who ask government for a

monopolistic position in the market—seeking to gain by the coercive elimination of would-be competitors. When successful in such depredations, they gain by denying others the opportunity to gain. Their gain is someone else's loss, a form of subsidy-slavery.

Reflect upon the countless subsidies being sought, not merely by the socialists but even by those who call themselves "free enterprisers." Each subsidy, when granted, gives birth to numerous regulations. Almost all of these regulations limit creative action, and they go far to explain our country's rapid decline into the Command Society—enslavement! Along with the enslavement occurs the deadening of private ownership, a fundamental feature of the free society.

The government type of enslavement grows out of at least three hallucinations:

(1) *I am wise!* With few exceptions, those wielding power over others are corrupted. Such authority tends to intoxicate them; they see others as fallible, but never themselves.

(2) *I am it!* Government controls what it subsidizes. Most of the 16,000,000 elected and appointed government officeholders think of themselves as the state. They come to believe that the dollars they use to subsidize are the government's dollars, and that they are the government.

(3) *I am omniscient!* This is the little-god syndrome. Be like me, do as I say, obey my edicts, and thou shall be graced with the good life.

The truth? Not a one of them is any more competent to direct our mortal moments than to direct our spirits in the Hereafter! This is to say that they can no more effectively direct creativity at the earthly level than they can direct Creation. Managing the creative lives of others is beyond any man's competence. But the wiseacres do not know this.

How then, are we to rid ourselves of these enslavements? There is only one answer: To be blessed with citizens—in office and out—who understand the limited role of government as did Grover Cleveland, and who will not deviate from their convictions.

13

OBLIGATIONS SPAWN MENTAL GROWTH

There is nothing so elastic as the human mind. Like imprisoned steam, the more it is pressed the more it rises to resist the pressure. The more we are obliged to do the more we are able to accomplish. **—TRYON EDWARDS**

The American theologian, Tryon Edwards (1809–94), expressed a truth, which like ever so many a truth is the opposite of what is found in the popular mythology. "Popular opinion is the greatest lie in the world," wrote Carlyle. The cause of this lie? Far more causes than we can count. Among them are *ambitions* in the derogatory sense: the seeking of fame, power, popularity, be-like-me-ness and so on. The millions who fall in this category are no more than followers of ignoble ambitions! They spawn no mental growth but, rather, assist the growing socialism which presently bedevils so much of the world. Let's speculate on how this can be corrected.

As a starter, ignore popular opinion. If righting mass notions were the solution to the mess we are in, a return to the freedom

58

way of life would be utterly hopeless. The restoration of freedom is not a numbers problem. We do not have to convert the masses; every good movement in all history has been led by an infinitesimal minority.

Aside from Jesus of Nazareth, whose movement started with only a handful of followers, the most outstanding example known to me was the accomplishment of a Venetian priest—Paolo Sarpi. Andrew Dickson White, co-founder and first President of Cornell University, wrote a book entitled *Seven Great Statesmen*. He accords first place to this priest. Sarpi alone initiated what proved to be one of the most beneficial movements in modern history—the separation of church and state.

The Papal Establishment in Rome at this time was, without exception, composed of power mongers—even murderers—and Venice was largely under its thumb. When Venice threw off this yoke it enjoyed a moral, political and an economic renascence. Father Paul—Sarpi—lived in Venice, then a nation, not just a city as now. The economic result? Venice became the greatest free-trade nation in the world up until that time.

For a remarkable illustration of how the separation of Church and State worked its wonders, observe how diametrically Leo III (Pope 1878–1903) differed from the power mongers 300 years earlier, prior to Sarpi's victory. Wrote this Pope: "It is the mind, or reason, which is the predominant element in us who are human creatures; it is this which renders a human being human, and distinguishes him essentially and generically from the brute."

Governmental behavior, if overextended, stifles economic progress, but if properly limited the law assures economic well-being. Reflect on the works of Frederic Bastiat (1801–50). I introduced his 79-page book, *The Law,* to our country in the early forties. It deals with the role of government—the political—

and with the advantages of freedom—economic progress. We at FEE have sold over 300,000 volumes of this book and ever so many of his larger works.

Those of us who believe in freedom have an obligation to so direct our lives and actions and stand responsible for the consequences. The American author, Elbert Hubbard (1859–1915), expressed a belief worthy of emulation: "I believe in freedom—social, economical, . . . political, mental and spiritual."

- Social: freedom of everyone—no exception—to act creatively as each pleases.
- Economical: freedom to produce whatever one pleases and to exchange mine for thine.
- Political: freedom from overextended government, with the law limited to keeping the peace and invoking a common justice.
- Mental: freedom to speak and write one's own convictions.
- Spiritual: freedom from the error that mortal man is the endower of our rights. The faith of freedom is ". . . that all men are . . . endowed by their Creator with certain unalienable Rights, that among these are Life, Liberty. . . ."

Wrote Stewart Edward White, a famous author and one of the greatest spiritual thinkers known to me: "A belief is not a possession until you can demonstrate its workability."

We at FEE have demonstrated over the past 34 years how freedom works its wonders, and so have ever so many others in various nations. Thus, millions possess a belief in freedom, but many are pessimistic about its recovery—mistakenly filled with gloom! Wrote that remarkable English statesman, Edmund Burke, in 1779:

How often has public calamity been arrested on the very brink of ruin, by the seasonable energy of a *single man?* Have we no such man amongst us? I am as sure as I am of my being, that *one* vigorous mind without office, without situation, without public functions of any kind, (at a time when the want of such a thing is felt, as I am sure it is) I say, *one* such man, confiding in the aid of God, and full of just reliance in his own fortitude, vigor, enterprise, and perseverance, would first draw to him *some few like himself,* and then that multitudes, hardly thought to be in existence, would appear and troop about him.

Interestingly, the millions who are presently trooping about the socialists are doing so unconsciously; and when that *one* exemplar of freedom appears, they will troop about him just as unconsciously. May that *one* man, confiding in the aid of God, be *the one you see in the mirror!*

14

OUR MUTUAL OBLIGATIONS

The man who never reads will never be read, he who never quotes will never be quoted; he who will not use the thoughts of other men's brains, proves he has no brains of his own.
—CHARLES H. SPURGEON

This English clergyman (1834–92), in the above, inspires some interesting reflections that relate to our mutual obligations and human liberty.

The man who never reads will never be read. "We may glean knowledge by reading, but we must separate the wheat from the chaff." A high percentage of reading material—newspapers, magazines and even books—classify as chaff. If self-improvement be one's objective, all reading should be over one's head, as the saying goes. That's the kind of material I aim to read. Very often I must read a sentence several times. Thinking required!

I am far from an authority on such a profound subject, so let me quote some of the all-time sages on the advantage of reading.

- A man of ability, for the chief of his reading, should select such works as he feels are beyond his own power to have produced. What can other books do for him but waste his time or augment his vanity? —*J. Foster*

- Reading is to the mind what exercise is to the body.
  —*Joseph Addison*

- To read without reflecting, is like eating without digesting.
  —*Edmund Burke*

- We should be as careful of the books we read, as of the company we keep. The dead very often have more power than the living. —*Tryon Edwards*

- It's what you read when you don't have to that determines what you will be when you can't help it. —*D. F. Potter*

- It is not wide reading but useful reading that tends to excellence. —*Aristippus*

. . . he who never quotes will never be quoted. I am unaware of anyone, past or present, whose writings have been featured by more quotations per book than mine! And this for certain: I am quoted far less frequently by other writers than the authors whose words I borrow! There are at least two reasons for this: (1) my lack of a wisdom comparable to theirs; and (2) the unpopular nature of my subject matter—explaining the freedom philosophy at a time when socialism is on the rampage.

Here is a Latin Proverb we should always keep in mind: *"Nothing is ever too often repeated that is not sufficiently learned."* Repetition is, indeed, the mother of learning!

The greatest of all earthly miracles, the freedom way of life, has not been sufficiently learned by anyone, its essence approximated only by a few. We should seek out these few, and make the best of their enlightened thoughts our own. Once these thoughts are digested, share with those who are potential devotees. Keep on quoting! The more one shares—gives—the more he or she learns. A Biblical truism: "It is more blessed to give than to receive." Hopefully, the listeners and/or readers will excel the givers!

There are excellent books by the wiser individuals throughout the ages—Confucius, Socrates, Burke, Emerson and hundreds of other men and women—available to those of us who seek enlightenment. These gems we quote, attracting others, becoming their mentors.

As one who believes in quoting the wise, here are a few samplings on this subject:

- He that recalls the attention of mankind to any part of learning which time has left behind it, may be truly said to advance the literature of his own age. —*Samuel Johnson*

- He presents me with what is always an acceptable gift who brings me news of a great thought before unknown. He enriches me without impoverishing himself.
  —*Christian Bovee*

- To select well among old things [ideas] is almost equal to inventing new ones. —*Nicholas Trublet*

- We are not always so composed, so full of wisdom, that we are able to take in at once the whole scope of a work according to its merit. Do we not mark in a book passages which seem to have a direct reference to ourselves? —*Goethe*

. . . **he who will not use the thoughts of other men's brains, proves he has no brains of his own.** There are two parts to the brain: (1) the diencephalon, possessed by higher animals and also by man and (2) the cortex, possessed only by human beings, endowing us with the capacity for abstract thought.

Assuredly Spurgeon's reference was to the disuse of the latter faculty. Wrote the famous biologist, Renee von Eulenburg-Wiener: "There also seem sufficient grounds for the assumption that a habitual disuse of these centers results or at least brings about a certain mental decline, and examples bearing on this contention are only too numerous."[1]

There are two or three billion individuals in this world of ours who have let themselves go to seed and, thus, fall in this woeful category. The problem of those of us who love liberty? We have a *mutual obligation* to assist each other. Here, in my view, is an appropriate prayer:

Thy blessings upon our freedom associates, near and far, past and present, that we may do thy will.

---

[1]See *Fearfully and Wonderfully Made* by Renee von Eulenburg-Wiener (New York: The Macmillan Company, 1938), p. 310.

15

THE ROLE OF GOALS

... and only a highly evolved man
is willing to defend the liberty of
others. —**LECOMTE DU NOÜY**

Dr. du Noüy (1883–1947), internationally known French scientist, author of *Human Destiny,* gave to posterity a valuable truth in that book. Most everyone wants liberty for self, but few there are who will defend the liberty of others. Short of such defense, there can be no liberty for anyone. Thus, those of us who love liberty have an obligation to evolve—grow in awareness, perception, consciousness—every day of our mortal lives.

Mankind's evolution is pre-ordained, as beautifully dramatized by Professor William Herbert Carruth (1859–1924):

> A fire-mist and a planet,
>   A crystal and a cell,
> A jellyfish and a saurian,
>   And caves where the cavemen dwell;
> Then a sense of law and beauty,
>   And a face turned from the clod—
> Some call it Evolution,
>   And others call it God.

Whether one's goal—this aim and aspiration—is high or low makes a tremendous difference. For as James Russell Lowell observed, "Not failure, but low aim is crime."

No one is immune to failure. To do one's best, without succeeding, is no crime. But to aim low, such as striving for wealth by theft, *is* a crime. Only a very small percentage of the population descend to this direct and open breaking of the Commandment, "Thou shalt not steal."

However, there are millions who get the government to steal for them—the actions range from food stamps to social security to medicare to replicas of the Gateway Arch by the thousands to more massive economic devastations than anyone can count. All of this is "financed" by a rapidly growing inflation—irredeemable paper money. These are low aims—crimes of the first order!

So let us be aware of the shameful and degrading consequences if our aim be low—our goal unworthy. This is step number one. The second step is to discover and reach for higher goals, to learn how to explain and live by them. Here is a wise observation by Joel Hawes: "Aim at the sun, and you may not reach it; but your arrow will fly far higher than if aimed at an object [ideal] on a level with yourself."

What is the lesson to be learned from this? See that one's aim is constantly ascending! Suppose I were to stop where I now am in explaining the freedom way of life. Stalemated! I am unaware of anyone who has more than scratched the surface in understanding and explaining Creation at the human level. Aim at the sun—this Heavenly Virtue—if you would emerge, grow, ascend!

Several thoughts which give excellent support to Joel Hawes, the American clergyman (1789–1867):

- Be always displeased with what thou art if thou desire to

attain to what thou art not, for where thou hast pleased thyself, there thou abidest.   —*Francis Quarles*

• High aims form high characters, and great objects bring out great minds.   —*Tryon Edwards*

• Have a purpose in life, and having it, throw into your work such strength of mind and muscle as God has given you.
                —*Thomas Carlyle*

• Dream manfully and nobly, and thy dreams shall be prophets.   —*E. G. Bulwer-Lytton*

• What are the aims which are at the same time duties? They are the perfecting of ourselves, and the happiness of others.
                —*Immanuel Kant*

• Providence has nothing good or high in store for one who does not resolutely aim at something high or good. A purpose is the eternal condition of success.   —*T. T. Munger*

• Aim at perfection in everything, though in most things it is unattainable; however, they who aim at it, and persevere, will come much nearer to it, then those whose laziness and despondency make them give it up as unattainable.
                —*Philip Chesterfield*

The above are examples of highly evolved men. Not only were they willing to defend the liberty of others but their method— self-improvement—was as right as right can be. Let us aim for the high and the good: *Liberty for one and all!*

16

THE VOICE OF CONSCIENCE

Cowardice asks, is it safe?
Expediency asks, is it politic?
Vanity asks, is it popular?
But Conscience asks, is it right?
—WILLIAM MORLEY PUNSHON

This English Wesleyan minister (1824–81), by his four questions, brilliantly emphasizes the virtue of conscience. And we should recall that "virtue" once meant excellence and power. George Washington exemplified such virtue and gave to his countrymen this sound advice: "Labor to keep alive in your heart that little spark of celestial fire called conscience."

This tiny spark of conscience must be identified and distinguished from the blazes of nonsense fanned by cowardice, expediency, and vanity.

Wrote Confucius: "To know what is right and not do it is the worst cowardice." Many Americans believe that freedom to act creatively as they please is right. However, they are too timid to stand ramrod straight for a way of life so at odds with popular jargon. This fear is not entirely unfounded. Jesus was crucified for his *holiness*. No one of us being remotely as pure as He, the worst that will beset us is disrespect—how awful! Each of us knows, deep down, that cowardice is far worse than public disdain.

Wrote the English poet, Percy B. Shelley (1792–1822):

> He was a coward to the strong;
> He was a tyrant to the weak.

Reflect on those who were cowards when they lived under such strong dictators as Hitler, Stalin and their ilk. But know-it-allness—the little god syndrome—is contagious. These very same cowards would become tyrants when and if an opportunity opened up to them. Take note of those in our homeland who fear to criticize our political power mongers, but who—when and if they get into office—will behave just as tyrannically. Wrote the English navigator, Sir Walter Raleigh (1552–1618): "Better it were not to live than to live a coward."

Expediency—the doing of what is to one's immediate advantage rather than what is right or just—is, indeed, *politic!* That word in old-English phrasing meant artful or crafty—*political* in its most derogatory sense. Wrote the American clergyman, Edwin Chapin (1814–80): "When private virtue is hazarded on the perilous cast of expediency, the pillars of the republic, however apparent their stability, are infected with decay at the very centre."

Expediency is akin to cowardice: (1) it stifles virtue, (2) it damages those who practice it, and (3) it corrupts the American Republic.

1—to be expedient is to lie, to take positions one knows to be false. It is to disobey the Commandment, "Thou shalt not bear false witness against thy neighbor." Expediency says, in effect: To hell with the heavenly virtues.

2—How does lying wreak its damage on those who lie? It

destroys character and rots the soul. Wrote the English Quaker and founder of Pennsylvania, William Penn (1644–1718): "When thou art obliged to speak, be sure to speak the truth; equivocation is half way to lying and lying is whole way to hell."

3—Expediency plays havoc with our Republic; only utter ignorance is more dangerous. Wrote Henry Ward Beecher: "Expedients are for an hour, but principles are for the ages." Those who do not heed principles either know them not or couldn't care less. Their deplorable tactic? An ignoble resort to such short-run, momentary "gains" as power, popularity, governmental handouts and the like. The unprincipled top the list as enemies of our Republic!

Vanity asks, is it popular? The Irish satirist and Dean of St. Patrick's Jonathan Swift (1667–1745) gave this topic a satirical "fly": "The strongest passions allow us some rest, but vanity keeps us perpetually in motion. What a dust do I raise! says the fly upon a coach-wheel. And at what a rate do I drive! says the fly on the horse's back."

Vanity is the quicksand of reason, which has little chance to function so long as vanity prevails. "The most violent passions have their intermissions; vanity alone gives us no respite." Wrote the Bard of Avon: "Vanity keeps persons in favor with themselves, who are out of favor with all others."

Here are five more thoughts by wise men on this intellectual weakness:

To be a man's own fool is bad enough, but the vain man is everybody's.   —*William Penn*

When a man has no longer any conception of excellence above his own, his voyage is done; he is dead; dead in the trespasses and sins of blear-eyed vanity.   —*Henry Ward Beecher*

There is no restraining men's tongues or pens when charged with a little vanity.   —*George Washington*

Great mischiefs happen more often from folly, meanness and vanity, than from the greater sins of avarice and ambition.
—*Edmund Burke*

Vanity is the foundation of the most ridiculous and contemptible vices—the vices of affectation and common lying.
—*Adam Smith*

Finally, how rid ourselves of cowardice, expediency and vanity? There is but one way: find the answer to what's right—the source of which is the individual's highest conscience!

As I see it, life's highest goal should be *growth* in awareness, perception, consciousness. Briefly, see how closely one's finite consciousness can approximate Infinite Consciousness.

In this respect, most people are unaware of their potentialities. To use Carl Jung's enlightened understanding and phrasing: "each of us has a partner—the undiscovered self." Discover thyself; there's a gold mine within thee! As Dr. Fritz Kunkel revealed to us: "*Immense hidden powers* lurk in the unconscious of the most common man—indeed, of all people without exception."

Let's repeat what the Father of our country gave us as a simple formula for the road to righteousness and a restoration of our Republic as "the home of the brave [no cowardice or expediency or vanity] and the land of the free":

Labor to keep alive in your heart that little spark of celestial fire called conscience!

17

THE EMERGENCE OF TRUTH

Ultimately with God's aid, Truth always emerges and finally prevails supreme in its power over the destiny of mankind, and terrible is the retribution for those who deny, defy, or betray it.
—VIRGIL JORDAN

The late Virgil Jordan was President of the National Industrial Conference Board when I joined the staff as Executive Vice-president in May 1945. As a scholar, writer, speaker and devotee of freedom he was one of the all-time greats!

In his search for Truth, my friend relied upon "God's aid," a faith which evokes hostility in some quarters, puzzlement in others. For clarification, I turn to my associate, Reverend Edmund Opitz:

> God, for many people, is a Cosmic Bell-Hop who is "up there" to run our celestial errands for us; or He's The Man Upstairs who'll do right by us if we butter him up. He's the Fond Uncle who hands out goodies and expects our praise in return. He's the Coach who brings us the big win, the Judge who punishes our enemies. And so on.

We begin our growing up out of these childish superstitions into the world vision of theism when we learn to think and act on the premise that a Creative Intelligence is at work in the universe. The immense variety of living forms testifies to the creativity, and the elegant adaptation of means to ends bespeaks intelligence. The Creative Intelligence is the universe's support system, and it fulfills its purpose throughout nature, in history, and above all by means of persons. The cosmos is rationally structured; it's a coherent whole, a universe. It follows that history has meaning, human life has a purpose, individuals count. To say "God exists" is to affirm that the whole show makes sense, and that by taking thought we may catch glimpses of the big pattern.

Human life does, indeed, have a purpose. But what of those who deny, defy, or betray life's highest purpose? In what manner is the retribution terrible?

In the above, my associate refers to "God" as "a Creative Intelligence." Wrote the Greek philosopher, Empedocles (490–430 B.C.): "God is a circle whose center is everywhere and its circumference nowhere." One may infer from this that we humans are finite centers and that our explorations can be no more than forward motions toward the Infinite. This is why my term for "God" is "Infinite Consciousness." This makes the comparison between infinite and finite easier. Now to those who defy God's Truth.

Consciousness is *the only* aspect of life that continues into the Hereafter—"the state of life after death." Our mortal moments are lived at their finest and highest when they include a preparation for Eternity.

The "terrible retribution that will bedevil those who deny, defy or betray this concept"? For the Materialist, these mortal moments are all there is to existence. There is *nothing* over and beyond our tiny, dormant, human "minds."

In a seminar discussion, the question arose, "I don't have to believe in God to believe in freedom do I?" My reply, "No, *you* do not have to believe in God to believe in freedom; but if there were no general belief in God—the Right beyond might—there would be no freedom!"

Imagine the situation if "we know-next-to-nothings" were regarded as the sole source of existence—no Creation, *no external source of Truth*. The retribution for those who defy is to face a pointless life—no Hereafter. And if all possessed a similar outlook there would be no meaningful human life on earth!

Unless there be an awareness of Creation and the Hereafter, wisdom in its highest sense is out of reach. Awareness of how little one knows is wisdom. For instance, if one were aware of how much he or she does not know—trillions times trillions of phenomena—that individual would be graced with an all-time wisdom. Socrates, regarded as one of the wisest, remarked: "That man thinks he knows everything, whereas he knows nothing. I, on the other hand, know nothing, but I know I know nothing." The more one knows, the greater is the unknown.

Socrates regarded himself as a philosophical midwife. He received from that *Source* over and beyond self and shared with all who cared to listen.

Wrote the American minister, Ralph Sockman: "The larger the island of knowledge, the longer the shoreline of wonder." The more we know the more we wonder, not only about the Heavenly unknown, but about its earthly offspring—the mysterious way freedom works its wonders.

18

ASPIRE TO SEE AFAR

*The genius of man is a continua-
tion of the power that made him
and that has not done making
him.* **—EMERSON**

The first question that must be asked and answered has to do with
first causes: What is this power that marshaled the physical,
chemical, biological and social forces that made every one of us?
The Scottish bookseller and compiler of a Bible Concordance,
Alexander Cruden (1701–70), gave an enlightening answer: "God
is one of the names which we give to that external, infinite, and
incomprehensible being, the creator of all things, who preserves
and governs everything by his almighty power and wisdom, and
who is the only object of our worship."

The multitudes do not grasp this. Ever so many people in this
and other lands know not the meaning of worship as used by
Cruden. I refer to those who "worship" wealth, fame, self-esteem, power to run the lives of others—those who *see* nothing
beyond their own little minds, who view themselves as the power
that made them. An Infinite Being to them is a mere figment of

the imagination. But enough about those who see not. My aim is to inquire into "the genius of man"—his inherent nature—hoping that more of us may find a motivating aspiration.

What did Emerson mean by "genius"? We must know the right answer if we are to aspire and see afar; only then will we have a motivating aspiration and attain an attracting exemplarity. According to the dictionary, genius is: "Great mental capacity . . . especially, great and original creative activity."

Here are four enlightening thoughts:

Genius, that power which dazzles mortal eyes is oft but perseverance in disguise. *—Henry Austin*

Genius is only a superior power of seeing. *—John Ruskin*

The first and last thing required of genius is the love of truth. *—Goethe*

Genius may be described as the spirit of discovery. It is the eye of intellect and the wing of thought. It is always in advance of its time—the pioneer for the generation which it precedes. *—William Simms*

Austin suggests that attainments that strike some as genius may be perseverance disguised, which implies that mere perseverance is not genius, although it may be a means to that lofty height. Here is an instance from the writings of Samuel Johnson, compiler of the first English dictionary: "Great works are performed, not by strength, but by perseverance. He that shall walk *with vigor,* three hours a day, will pass, in seven years, a space equal to the circumference of the globe." Such a stunt (over 24,000 miles!) does not betoken genius. Anyone who would do such would be an all-time physical marvel, but no sensible person would ever attempt such a venture.

To discover those who qualify as geniuses, let Johnson's metaphorical impossibility serve as a suggestion for what *is* possible in the intellectual, moral and spiritual realm—the road to freedom. Here are three interesting observations:

- Nothing is so hard but search will find it out.

  —Robert Herrick

- Never despair, but if you do, work in despair.

  —Edmund Burke

- I'm proof against that word failure. I've seen behind it. The only failure a man ought to fear is failure in cleaving to the purpose he sees to be best.   *—Mary Ann Evans*

While there are numerous others—past and present—I am unaware of any genius who better grasped the power that made man and that has not done making him than Ralph Waldo Emerson. A great exemplar!

Nothing is so hard but search will find it out. Were this the qualification for becoming a genius, there never has been nor will there ever be such an individaal. No finite person in all history, regardless of how hard the search, has known what Infinite Consciousness is. Know error to find the truth!

How become a genius? One way is to search in the realm of one's uniqueness. Who knows what the reward will be! An awareness of an *incomprehensible* being will assuredly grace a few. Mortal life has no higher gift!

Never despair, but if you do, work in despair. And enlist your understanding by recalling the words of a thoughtful philosopher: "What we call despair is often the painful eagerness of unfed hope." Most of us have hopes—high aspirations—but ever so many let it go at that. Their hopes waste away, unnourished.

Having failed to grasp the upgrading truth that the art of becoming is composed of acts of overcoming, they yield to discouragement—and that's painful.

Those who perceive life's purpose aright will never be stalemated at the desperation level. They will courageously rise to the challenge.

Burke knew the remedy—work out your despair! Jeremy Taylor added his wisdom: "It is impossible for that man to despair who remembers that his Helper is omnipotent." Our Helper is not only omnipotent but is *The Source!*

Wrote the English novelist, Mary Ann Evans (1819–80): *I'm proof against that word failure. I've seen behind it. The only failure a man ought to fear is failure in cleaving to the purpose he sees to be best.*

There is more to failure than meets the eye. To see only the failure is to be beaten, discouraged, filled with bitterness and despair. But to see "behind it" is to know what went wrong and why.

Millions of Americans are distraught by the consequences of our decline into socialism. They see dollars losing value as prices mount. And they tend to blame the suppliers of goods and services for those higher prices—a failure of private enterprise! They do not see "behind it" to the reckless government spending and debt-based printing of worthless paper money.

Until we more clearly see and relate cause and consequence, see that it is the socialistic measures which have failed, we must bear those dreadful consequences. Once we understand, we may turn from the socialism that fails, return to the success that follows a faith in the market economy.

Where lies our hope? The power to make us, as Emerson wrote, is not done making us. Faith in this Truth is absolutely essential if freedom is to prevail. Three thoughts we should keep in mind:

> Faith makes the discords of the present the harmonies of the future.   —*Robert Collyer*

> Despotism may govern without faith but Liberty cannot.
> —*Alexis de Tocqueville*

> Miracle is the darling child of faith.   —*Goethe*

19

FROM THE "KNOWN" TO THE UNKNOWN

This is the world of seeds; of causes and of tendencies; The other is the world of harvests and of perfected consequences.
—JOSEPH ADDISON

Wrote the German humorist, poet and statesman, Jean Paul Richter (1763–1826): "If there were no future life, our souls would thirst for it." Of all the adults on this earth, how many *thirst* for a future life, a life after our earthly life is done? No one can even guess the number; however, it is possible and perhaps enlightening to open up this question and speculate on several generalities.

Let's first reflect on the world of the "known." Ever so many of the ills in today's world originate in the millions who "think" they can get along without drawing and relying on the Creation which brought them into being—to me, an absurdity!

These individuals suffer as they would if deprived of many other ingredients of life. While readily admitting that they cannot live without food, drink, red blood cells or brain, these poor souls believe they can survive on those infinitesimal talents which they alone possess. These millions see no need to come to terms with the power which created them! When mankind is afflicted with such egotism, a good society is out of the question!

Egotism or egoism is: "constant, excessive reference to oneself in speaking or writing; self-conceit." Wrote E. K. Goldthwaite: "Overstuffed egos, waddling about in self-appointed importance." These politico-economic "waddlers"—those who "know"—compose a large percentage of the population. For whom do they vote? For politicians who will "waddle" for them at the expense of others!

In the same lamentable category are those who avow their atheism—nothing in the Cosmos above their finite minds. Wrote the American lawyer, John Foster (1836–1917): "The atheist is one of the most daring beings in creation, a contemner [scorner] of God who explodes his laws by denying his existence."

A given individual may affirm his belief in freedom, while at the same time denying any belief in *The Source:* God, Infinite Consciousness, *Creation.* However, if everyone in the society were atheist, there could not be a free society. Everything in Nature, be it good or evil, has its source. Freedom is good—creation at the human level—and its Source *is* Creation!

In addition to the millions who deny *The Source,* there are scores of millions who have no beliefs whatsoever concerning this matter—afflicted by blindness. In Matthew 15:14 we read: "They be blind leaders of the blind. And if the blind lead the blind, both shall fall into the ditch."

The number of people in these categories—the know-it-alls, the atheists, the blind—is so great that all nations appear to be falling into the ditch. Disaster? Not if we can find the remedy!

And it isn't easy, for the more affluent a people become, as in the U.S.A., the greater is the tendency for talents to lie dormant. But is this the way it must be? Negative! It requires a *renewal* of the best thinking ever to grace humanity!

Let us now reflect on the "Unknown"—*The Source*. No one knows what it is; only a few know that it is. Wrote that remarkable author, Stewart Edward White: "You've got to play with the idea before you can make it work, because you are not operating in your accustomed substance. You are employing a higher creative form which you don't know how to use except unconsciously and relaxedly." To even move in the direction of the Unknown—The Source—cannot result from a personal commandment. The Unknown must indeed be approached "relaxedly," that is, *joyously!*

The English essayist, poet and statesman, Joseph Addison (1672–1719), in writing about the life to come—the hereafter— claims that it "is the world of harvests and of perfected consequences." Briefly, the harvest in the world to come is determined by the perfection achieved in our mortal moments. Wrote the English courtier, orator and wit, Philip Chesterfield (1694–1778): "Aim at perfection in everything, though in most things it is unattainable. However, they who aim at it, and persevere, will come much nearer to it than those whose laziness and despondency make them give it up as unattainable."

The above is excellent but, in my judgment, his "though in most things it is unattainable," goes too far. Wrote Tryon Edwards: "Much of the glory and sublimity of truth is connected with its mystery. To understand *everything* we must be like God." Even this I would modify to read: "To understand *anything* we must be like God." Truth and nothing but the truth exists only in *The Source,* unattainable by any human being. It is important that we properly evaluate our *impotence* in order to avoid the horrible and all-too-common assessment of self: *omnipotence!*

Once our limitations are properly evaluated, there follows an understanding of the efficacy of the free and unfettered market—our tiny and varying bits of thoughts and skills freely flowing and configurating. Result? Growth in material well-being and plenty of time to grow in consciousness—which should be our highest aim in life.

Here is a thought worthy of deep reflection by the Hungarian patriot, Louis Kossuth (1802–94): "The cause of freedom is identified with the destinies of humanity, and in whatever part of the world it gains ground, by and by it will be a common gain to all who desire it." Here we have the case for exemplarity. Let us in the U.S.A. set the example for freedom and "by and by it will be a common gain for all who desire it." Great thinkers over the ages have passed on to us the best of all methods for personal and societal advancement:

There is a transcendent power in example. We reform others unconsciously, when we walk uprightly. —*Madam Swetchine*

People seldom improve when they have no model but themselves to copy after. —*Oliver Goldsmith*

Nothing is so infectious as example. —*Charles Kingsley*

We can do more good by being good, than in any other way. —*Rowland Hill*

Example is the school of mankind. They will learn at no other. —*Edmund Burke*

So act that your principle of action might safely be made a law for the whole world. —*Immanuel Kant*

Much more gracious and profitable is doctrine by example, than by rule.   *—Herbert Spencer*

Of all commentaries upon the Scripture, good examples are the best and the liveliest.   *—John Donne*

Wrote the Sage of Concord: "There is a persuasion in the soul of man that he is here for a cause, and that he was put down in this place by the *Creator* to do the work for which He inspired him; that thus he is an over-match for all the antagonists that could contrive against him."

Let us ardently strive to learn more and more of the Unknown. What will be the reward? *Freedom will grace our lives!*

20
THE MASTERS OF VICTORY

The nerve which never relaxes
The eye which never blanches
The thought which never wavers
These are the masters of victory.
—AUTHOR UNKNOWN

It is a safe guess that many of the wisest statements ever uttered are unknown to anyone in our time, for all people make remarks no one remembers—not even themselves. All the more reason, then, to cherish the proverbial wisdom we do possess. "It is better to verify the proverb, and take everything unknown as magnificent," wrote Leigh Hunt, "rather than to predetermine it as worthless." We know not who authored "The Masters of Victory" or when it was written. But it is, indeed, magnificent and the four points deserve reflection that we may profit from their wisdom.

The word "nerve" has numerous definitions but the one mentioned above has to be this: "emotional control; coolness in danger; courage."

Emotional control: Ever so many of us lack emotional control. We are distraught when listening to or reading bad news, totally

86

unaware of all the good that goes on. To assert that the latter is a million times greater than the former would be an understatement. On the other hand, we are elated by all sorts of trivia ranging from flattery to the election of a favorite politician. Aim to possess the nerve which never relaxes—steadfast for high ideals such as freedom—if thou wouldst be featured by *nerve*.

Coolness in danger: One of my brilliant friends humorously phrased this point: "All of life is filled with woe and strife and few of us get out of it alive." Of course, no one survives this earthly life. But those who fret about what may happen—earthquakes, wars, cancer, heart attacks, depressions, old-age, poverty and countless other scary dangers—induce *stress,* which dramatically shortens life. The ones best gifted with coolness look upon birth and death as parts of the Divine Plan—our mortal moments being a passing and heavenly delight rather than a few years of hellish doom. Hail to those graced with coolness!

Courage: Confucius said, "To see what is right and not do it is a lack of courage." Many citizens know it is everyone's right to act creatively as he or she pleases. However, if a creative action is unpopular, such as hiring youngsters, freely exchanging goods and services with people in other countries, educating one's own children, or ever so many contradictions of governmental or trade union interventions, they lack the courage to stand for what they believe to be right.

Wrote the clergyman, James F. Clarke (1820–88): "Conscience is the root of all courage; if a man would be brave, *let him obey his conscience.*" For freedom to prevail, there must be more men and women graced with courage!

In beginning this, the second point, by our Unknown Author, I find that he or she was among the ancients. I attempted to interpret what was meant by "The eye that never blanches," for that word in our present vocabulary doesn't make much sense in this context. But the dictionary does give an *archaic* meaning for "Blanch": "Shrink, give way," one meaning of the latter being "betray." In our phrasing, the line would read, "The eye that never waivers or betrays"—a strict adherence to what one's conscience dictates as righteous!

It is possible that our Author was familiar with that brilliant thought expressed 2,000 years ago: "The light of the body is in the eye; if therefore thine eye be single, the whole body shall be full of light." (Matthew 6:22) The light of the body is truth, wisdom, enlightenment—perception! Refer to Webster for the definition of "single": "Not deceitful or artful, simple, honest, sincere." Shakespeare used the word in this same sense: "I speak with a single heart."

Single is directly linked to *integer,* meaning "whole, entire, not divided." Contrasted to *single* is *double,* which has the same original root as "duplicity." Such phrases as "double dealing" and "double talk" convey this connotation. *Integrity* is related to *integer,* and *single* as here used does, indeed, refer to *integrity!*

Let the eye be single and cast on improvement—whatever the endeavor—and improvement is bound to follow. One of countless examples was cited by Andrew Dickson White in his remarkable little book, *Fiat Money Inflation in France*. It had to do with that Frenchman, Brillat-Savarin, who was not only the founder of modern cookery but also a staunch classical liberal, while at the same time a member of the National Assembly: "Singular, that the man, Brillat-Savarin, who so fearlessly stood against this tide of unreason has left to the world simply a reputation as the most brilliant cook that ever existed." If the eye be cast aright—toward freedom—disregard fickle reputations. Such persons are the masters of victory.

Why applaud the thought which never wavers? To waver means "to show doubt or indecision . . . vacillate . . . to become unsteady." One's ambition should be to rid himself of such faults or foibles. The American theologian, John M. Mason (1770–89) shed light on the difficulty: "The wise man has foibles as well as the fool. Those of the one are known to himself, and concealed from the world; while those of the other are known to the world and concealed from himself."

The thoughts of those who never waver, who stand ramrod straight for right principles, live on forever, testimony to which was given by that remarkable Scottish poet, Charles McKay (1814–89): "The old thoughts never die; immortal dreams outlive their dreamers and are ours for aye; no thought once formed and uttered ever can expire."

May the thoughts we form and utter on behalf of freedom be helpful to *all* oncoming generations. Such intellectual, moral and spiritual ascendancy will qualify us as *the masters of victory*.

21

THE POWER OF THINKING JOYOUSLY

He is a wise man who does not grieve for the things he has not, but rejoices for those which he has. —**EPICTETUS**

One of the greatest philosophers of all time was Epictetus, a Roman slave, exiled with many other philosophers by Emperor Domitian who ruled 81–96 A.D. This Emperor was one of Rome's worst despots. His life was filled with grievances for the things he had not. Thank goodness he is all but forgotten. Epictetus, the slave, lived a life of joy for things which he had—righteous ideas. As a consequence, his works have had an enormous influence on western civilization. Thank goodness he is not forgotten.

Epictetus gained fame as a Stoic: "a Greek school of philosophy founded by Zeno about 308 B.C.: The Stoics believed that all happenings were the result of divine will and that therefore man should be calmly accepting and free from passion or joy.'' Epictetus differed in one respect, namely, to *rejoice* in what one has!

The philosophy of Epictetus is brought to us in *The Enchiridion*. Albert Solomon's introduction to the book sets the stage for this thesis: ''Roman Stoicism had been recognized the redeeming power of philosophical reason in all the moral and social purposes of life. Philosophy as a way of life makes men free. It is the last ditch stand of liberty in a world of servitude.''[1]

We who are interested in the freedom of individuals should *know* the meaning of philosophy as here used. According to my dictionary, philosophy is: ''A study of the processes governing thought and conduct; theory or investigation of the principles of law that regulate the universe and underlie all knowledge and reality . . . a study of human morals, character and behavior.''

Our exiled slave, having the reputation of a philosopher par excellence, went to Nicopolis, a small village far to the northeast of Athens and, of course, a long way from Rome. Hear this: ''He was so well regarded and highly esteemed that he established the reputation of the place as the town of Epictetus' School. Students came from Athens and Rome to attend his classes. Private citizens came to ask his advice and guidance.''[2]

Wrote the Roman statesman and Stoic philosopher, Marcus Aurelius (121–180 A.D.): ''The soul becomes dyed with the color of its thoughts.''

Epictetus gave to us the perfect methodological formula for a return to the freedom way of life. Using the above metaphor, what was the ''color'' of his thoughts? Self-improvement! Epic-

---

[1]See *The Enchiridion* by Epictetus (Indianapolis: The Bobbs-Merrill Company, Inc., 1955), p. 7.

[2]*Ibid.*, p. 9.

tetus as a teaching philosopher relied *exclusively* on the law of attraction. Consistent with this method is an old English maxim: "It is light that brings forth the eye." Excellence in any field, be it cooking, golf, liberty or whatever, is magnetic and is in tune with the Universal Law of Attraction. Here is what the distinguished scientist, Anthony Standen, had to say:

> All the phenomena of astronomy, which had baffled the acutest minds since the dawn of history, the movement of the heavens, of the sun and the moon, the very complex movements of the planets, suddenly tumble together and become intelligible in terms of the one staggering assumption, this *mysterious "attractive force."* And not only the movements of the heavenly bodies, far more than that, the movements of earthly bodies too are seen to be subject to the same mathematically definable law, instead of being, as they were for all previous philosophers, mere unpredictable happen-so's.[3]

While Standen may not have had human beings in mind when referring to "earthly bodies," the Law of Attraction works on us as irrevocably as on any item in nature. We are drawn to great enlightenment just as physical bodies are attracted by gravitation.

Let me cite a personal experience to demonstrate how the enlightenment of our exiled slave influenced my life. Some years ago I sent an article of mine to a remarkable thinker and writer in Montreal. Later, on the phone to me, he said, "What you have written sounds like the ideas in *The Enchiridion* by Epictetus." My reply: "I have never heard of the publication or the author. Please send me a copy." After reading this 39-page pamphlet, the light dawned—an explanation of why my ideas were similar to those of the ancient Stoic. Here it is.

---

[3]See *Science Is a Sacred Cow* by Anthony Standen (New York: E. P. Dutton & Company, Inc., 1950), pp. 63–64.

Epictetus did no writing—only thinking and explaining his ideas. Among his students was a young Roman, Flavius Arrian, who took courses at Nicopolis when Epictetus was elderly. Their informal discourses convinced Arrian that he had finally discovered a Stoic Socrates or a Stoic Diogenes, *who was not merely teaching a doctrine, but also living the truth.*

From the notes Arrian had taken, he published *The Enchiridion,* a brief summary of the basic ideas of Stoic philosophy and an introduction to the techniques required to transform Stoic philosophy into a way of life. Moral philosophy was first and foremost. A brilliant quote from this masterpiece has to do with what is, and what is not, within our power: "In our power are our thinking, our intentions, our desires, our decisions. These make it possible for us to control ourselves and to make of ourselves elements and parts of the universe, of nature. This knowledge of ourselves *makes us free in a world of dependencies.* This superiority of our power enables us to live in conformity with nature."

The Enchiridion was translated into numerous languages. "There were many outstanding bishops in the Catholic and Anglican Churches who were eager to transform the tradition of Roman Stoicism into Christian Stoicism. Among the Calvinistic denominations were many thinkers who were in sympathy with Stoic moral principles because of their praise of the austerity of life and of the control of passions." However, it was the following which explains why I, who had never heard of Epictetus, have been learning from him *unknowingly:* ". . . there is a continuous renascence of Stoicism from Descartes, Grotius, and Bishop Butler, to Montesquieu, Adam Smith and Kant. In this long development in modern times, the tiny *Enchiridion* of Epictetus played a remarkable part."

Imagine the enlightenment of one man projecting itself into the consciousness of such remarkable individuals as Adam Smith and Immanuel Kant—*seventeen centuries* later!

Being intimately familiar with the works of Adam Smith and Kant, here I am *two centuries* after their time, the recipient of the wisdom that originated in an exiled slave!

Three of many excellent thoughts in *The Enchiridion* we might well keep in mind:

- If anyone tells you that a certain person speaks ill of you, do not make excuses about what is said of you, but answer: "He was ignorant of my other faults, else he would not have mentioned these alone."
- When you do anything from a clear judgment that it ought to be done, never shrink from being seen to do it, even though the world should misunderstand it; for if you are not acting rightly, shun the action itself; if you are, why fear those who wrongly censure you?
- If you have assumed any character beyond your strength, you have both demeaned yourself ill in that *and quitted one which you might have supported.*

The lesson we should learn from our wondrous slave? Everlastingly strive for a light so brilliant that it will glow into the distant future—enlightening others. This is not only the joyous life but attests to the fact: *It is light that brings forth the eye!*

22

THOUGHTS: DEAD OR ALIVE?

Thought must take the stupen-
dous step of passing into
realization. **—EMERSON**

One reason why most individuals never realize their potentialities—remain at the dormant level—is that their thoughts die at
birth. Thoughts, in a way, are comparable to dreams—evanes-
cent—gone with the wind, as we say. Everyone has had countless
dreams. Remembered? We can remember having had them but
only in exceptional cases what they were. So what! But thoughts
must be captured and reflected upon at the moment of reception
if they are to advance into realization.

I am unaware of anyone who put his thoughts, conversations
and lectures into writing more conscientiously than the Sage of
Concord. The brilliant Newton Dillaway, whose intellectual and
spiritual hero was Emerson, spent years in condensing this sage's
works into a remarkable book, *The Gospel of Emerson.*[1]

---

[1]Unity Books, Unity Village, Missouri, 128 pp.

Henry Hazlitt, one of the great authors and exponents of freedom of our time, has emphasized again and again that a thought must be written out immediately on reception if it is not to be lost. This discipline, in no small measure, accounts for Hazlitt's expertise.

For the past 29 years I have kept a daily Journal. Every worthwhile thought of my own or others that came to me has been instantly recorded. Here is my joyful discipline: I will read every page from the beginning to the present—now about 2,000,000 words—and, when finished, start over again. The reward? There are literally thousands of forgotten thoughts, many of which are inspirations for an improved phrasing of the freedom thesis. Is this not a stupendous step toward realizing my potential? Emerson and Hazlitt would give me an "A" for effort—if not for accomplishment.

Emerson, one of my all-time favorites and the inspiration for this little essay, wrote these words of wisdom: "The genius of man is a continuation of the Power that made him and that has not done making him." These are the words Emerson used to identify this Power: God, The Universal Mind, The Creator of Man, Best Counsel, Supreme Spirit and, among others, Immense Intelligence. It is the latter I have used many times, for it relates accurately to thought reception: "We lie in the lap of *Immense Intelligence* which makes us receivers [perceivers] of its truth and organs of its activity. When we discern justice, when we discern truth, we do nothing of ourselves but allow a passage of its beams."

In order to do nothing of ourselves but allow a passage of its beams, we must develop a remarkable spirit. Why? The highest and most difficult of all human attainments is the discernment of justice and truth. The English essayist, Joseph Addison

(1672–1719) had this to say about justice: "To be perfectly just is an attribute of the divine nature; to be so to the utmost of our abilities, is the glory of man." And the American theologian, Tryon Edwards (1800–94), reminds us of the divine nature of truth: "Much of the glory and sublimity of truth is connected with its mystery. To understand everything we must be as God."

Justice is, indeed, an attribute of Divine Providence, and glory may be ascribed to individuals only to the extent that they are perfectly just in their thoughts and actions as related to their fellowmen. "Justice without wisdom is impossible," wrote J. A. Froude. Only living thoughts are wise, and only then is glory an earned encomium. Required for a growth in consciousness—life's purpose? Avoid dead thoughts!

As to the glory and sublimity of truth, all is mystery—no exception, none whatsoever. To dramatize this point, try to answer the question, "Who am I?"

Here is an infinitesimal part of the answer: I am one octillion atoms—1,000,000,000,000,000,000,000,000,000. These come and go at one quintillion—1,000,000,000,000,000,000—every second. Thus, I am a different person than a second ago. What is an atom? We know *that* it is but not *what* it is. This, and all else in Creation, is mystery! The recognition of this fact is the first steppingstone to truth. Why? We must know how little we know in order to know more than we now know!

The genius of man is, indeed, a continuation of the Power that made him *and that has not done making him*. Reflect on how little we now know, compared to all there is to be known. Reflect further on the enormous knowledge we now possess as compared to that of Cro-Magnon man 35,000 years ago. The Power—Creation—that made us what we are is still at work. Mankind 35,000 years in the future will, I believe, be as far ahead of us as we are ahead of our ancient ancestry. This is implicit in the evolutionary process!

Freedom from the know-it-alls—political and otherwise—is the momentous first step, if our high aim is to be realized. Wrote Tryon Edwards: "High aims form high characters and great objects bring out great minds." Each of us is the architect of his own character. *For freedom's sake, and our own, let us be great architects!*

23

COUNT OUR BLESSINGS, NOT MISERIES

*Blessings we enjoy daily, and for
the most part of them, because
they are so common, men forget
to pay their praises.*
—IZAAK WALTON

There are ever so many freedom devotees who are afflicted with downheartedness. Their pessimism is due to the political skulduggery—"rascality; trickery"—that features our present decline into socialism.

What possibly is the remedy for those who thus suffer? The ability to look in two directions at once! For, as Joseph Addison wrote: "A misery is not to be measured from the nature of an evil, but from the temper of the sufferer." Assuredly, we need to see the evil but, at the same time, see the good: our blessings—thousands of times greater. We *can* discipline ourselves to take a balanced view.

99

Good and bad have existed together since the beginning of time, but no one needs to wallow in the bad! I do not listen to or read the bad which, with few exceptions, is all the media reports. Does this selectiveness leave me unaware of the bad—our decline into socialism? Not at all! True, I miss the trivia—who murdered whom, political misdemeanors, or whatever—but not the over-all slump. I am as much aware of that as are those captivated by the trivia. Result? I have that much more time to think about what's right and to count my blessings; joy instead of despondency!

The English author, Izaak Walton (1593–1683) emphasized one of the most important characteristics of our all-too-human behavior, namely, that our blessings are so common that we forget to praise them, that is, to count them! This accounts for ever so many forms of personal and societal decadence.

The original source of the American miracle was our Declaration—unseating government as the source of human rights and placing the Creator there. The companion documents—the Constitution and the Bill of Rights—limited government more than ever before in history! Result? Americans looked to themselves rather than to government for welfare. Self-responsibility on an unprecedented scale! The millions enjoying blessings by the millions!

What happened after decades of countless blessings? The Source forgotten! And why? The blessings have become so abundant that today's citizens take them for granted; feeling no more gratitude for them than for the natural blessings of sunshine or the air we breathe.

There is, also, a very important reason for counting our blessings: it helps rid the soul of covetousness. To count one's blessings is to accent what's right, a truth rarely recognized as an inclusion in the infinite realm of righteousness. Why? Because covetousness is seldom evaluated as a wrong, even by those who repeat the Commandment, "Thou shalt not covet."

While some may deplore covetousness, few will regard it as an evil on the scale of murder, theft, and adultery. Nor will they think of it as having any relationship to our present politico-economic decline. This may be due to the fact that "Thou shalt not covet" is the last of the Ten Commandments and regarded, therefore, as the least important. Admittedly, a guess on my part.

I suspect that the ordering of the Commandments had nothing to do with a sin-grading scheme. Only one of the ten had obvious priority and it became the First Commandment. The other nine were listed, perhaps as they came to mind. And covetousness, more subtle and an afterthought, concludes the list. But, on reflection, covetousness is as deadly as any of the other sins— indeed, it tends to induce the others.

Covetousness or envy generates a destructive radiation with ill effect on all it touches.

Psychosomatic illness can be traced as much to envy as to hate, anger, worry, despondency.

But consider the social implications, the effects of envy on others. At first blush, the rich man appears not to be harmed because another covets his wealth. Envy, however, is not a benign, dormant element of the psyche; it has the same intensive force as rage, and a great deal of wisdom is required to put it down. Where understanding and self-control are wholly lacking, the weakling will resort to thievery, embezzlement, piracy, even murder, to gratify his envy and "get his share."

Though weakness of character afflicts all of us to some extent, only a few are so lacking in restraining forces as to personally employ naked force, such as thievery, to realize the objects of envy. Fear of apprehension and reprisal tends to hold such open-faced evil in check.

However, if the evil act can be screened, if the sense of personal guilt and responsibility can be sufficiently submerged, that is, if self-delusion can be effected, gratification of covetousness will be pursued by the "best people."

The way is no secret: achieve anonymity in a mob, committee, organization, society, or hide behind legality or majority vote.

With the fear of exposure removed, millions of Americans feather their own nests at the expense of others, and on a scale never imagined by thieves, pirates, or embezzlers. Our "best people," including the highly "educated," gratify their envy with no qualms whatsoever. But their salved conscience in no way lessens the evil of covetousness; quite the contrary, it emphasizes to us how powerfully this evil operates at the politico-economic level. This subtle evil is indeed the genesis of more obvious sins.

We should also note the extent to which this "guiltless" taking of property by coercion is rationalized. Accomplices, bearing such titles as philosophers and economists, rise to the occasion; they explain how the popular depredations are good to everyone, even for those looted. Thus, we find that covetousness, unchecked in the individual, lies at the root of the decline and fall of nations and civilizations.

In considering the effect on the one who covets, we must be careful not to confuse the taking of another's property with the taking unto oneself of a higher level of intelligence and morality exemplified by another. The former is depredation, harmful to both self and the other; the latter is emulation, helpful to all concerned.

As contrasted with the emulation of virtues, which takes nothing from but adds to the welfare of others, envy is nothing more than an avaricious greed to possess what exclusively belongs to others. Envy is a lust of the flesh as opposed to an elevation of the spirit. The Hindus saw it clearly for what it really is: "Sin is not the violation of a law or a convention but . . . ignorance . . . which seeks its own private gain at the expense of others." William Penn grasped this point: "Covetousness is the greatest of Monsters, as well as the root of all Evil."

As a person cannot be in two places at the same time, so is it impossible for the eye to be cast covetously at the material possessions of others and cast aspiringly at one's own creativity. Thus, envy leaves unattended the human being's upgrading; it is a positive distraction from the "hatching" process—Creation's Purpose. It's either hatch or rot, as with an egg; envy leaves the soul, the spirit, the intellect, the psyche to rot, and there can be no greater evil than this.

When it is clear that covetousness thwarts Creation's purpose and, thus, man's destiny—that among the cardinal sins none is greater—it surely behooves each of us to find a way to rid himself of this evil.

I believe the way is simply to proclaim: *Count your blessings!*

Any person who is not aware of countless blessings, regardless of how low or high his estate, will be no more aware of his blessings should his envy be gratified. Awareness of blessings is a state of consciousness and is not necessarily related to abundance and affluence. He who is rich in worldly goods but unaware of his blessings is poor, and probably covetous; he who is poor in worldly goods but aware of his blessings is rich, and assuredly without envy.

How easy the advice: Count your blessings! But what about the person unaware of his blessings? As well advise him to acquire wisdom, for wisdom *is* awareness. Some individuals are aware of no blessings, others of a few, still others of numerous blessings. Yet, no one is more than slightly aware, just as no one is more than slightly wise.

Exactly how unaware we are of our blessings can be seen by committing them to paper—actually counting. While they are in infinite supply, observe how few are recognized. Now, throw the list away; for these must be alive and every day in the consciousness, not stored on paper, not mechanically canned.

Try again, later: this is an exercise that one should never abandon. The list is longer! Note, also, how much greater the wisdom is. Conscious effort, really trying, constantly pressing against the unknown for more light is the nature of this discipline.

As progress is made in an awareness of our blessings, we are struck by how greatly they outnumber our woes and troubles. In a state of unawareness, the woes loom enormous, and we tend to covetousness; in awareness the woes are but trifles, and the covetousness fades away.

This remarkable cure for covetousness also puts us on the road to social felicity; for we best serve ourselves and others through the exercise of *self-responsibility and freedom!*

24

REAPING THE BLESSINGS OF FREEDOM

*Those who would expect to reap
the blessings of freedom must undergo the fatigue of supporting
it.* **—THOMAS PAINE**

Thomas Paine (1737–1809) played a vital role during the years of our Republic's founding. He was born in England and emigrated to America in 1774. His *Common Sense,* published in January 1776, is credited as having "had a tremendous effect in helping to bring about the Declaration of Independence." Anyone who thus contributes to the greatest political document of all time deserves our respect and appreciation.

In the above excellent quote, I would substitute the word "labor" for "fatigue." Fatigue sometimes implies ". . . mental exhaustion; weariness; it causes a mental decomposition of the . . . nerve cells." Working in freedom's vineyard must yield joy; no mentally exhausted individual can lend a hand in reaping the blessings of freedom. This noble objective can be aided and abetted only by those who find it a *joyous* pursuit. Have fun or forget it!

Those who work effectively on behalf of freedom do so as a labor of love—a joyous adventure toward the societal ideal. Wrote the English critic, John Ruskin (1819–1900): "It is only by labor that thought can be made healthy, and only by thought that labor can be made happy [joyous]; and the two cannot be separated with impunity."

It takes thoughts of the highest order—healthy thinking—to perceive the hellishness of socialism and comprehend the heavenly blessings of freedom. From darkness to light! However, there cannot be any great thoughts without joyous labor. The two are inseparable.

The freedom way of life demands creative thinkers. Creative thought is always joyous, but many obstacles stand in its way. Unless these obstacles be overcome freedom is stalemated—a mere pipe dream! Those thus victimized go through life as mere sleepwalkers. So let us identify and deal with some of these obstacles.

Lethargy—"indifference; apathy"—may head the list. Forget the millions who couldn't care less; reflect on the few who believe in freedom but are afflicted with apathy and thus are do-nothings. Why this dormancy—inaction?

The do-nothings look at the socialistic mess into which we are drifting and conclude that there is no hope of recovery. The error? Contrary to their estimate of the situation, they do not really know what is going on—nor does anyone else! No one knows what is going to happen in the *next* minute. It is easily demonstrable that no one knows anywhere near a trillionth of what happened in the *last* minute. An old saying raises this enlightening question: "How can you pretend to foretell the affairs of others when you cannot foresee your own?"

The remedy for this intellectual delinquency is to recognize that a Divine Source, over and beyond the mind of man, is in charge of human destiny. No human authority is in charge, nor is any collective able to perform such a role, or even to foretell its rhythmic devolution/evolution performance. May more of our brethren than now come to a recognition of this simple truth!

Cowardice ranks close to lethargy as a deterrent to freedom— and I speak here of moral cowardice. Many citizens in all walks of life suffer this frailty or weakness in some degree. They may be physically brave, but they are cowards in the sense of fearing to speak the truth as they see it.

I know many politicians who speak or write, not as they themselves assess truth but, rather, to gain popularity. They seek to align themselves with this group of voters while avoiding offense to that group. Truth is a casualty in their drive to get elected.

Reflect on the many who insist that freedom must be restored *gradually,* never all at once. Follow this dubious advice and feedom would never be restored! In 1946 I gave a lecture entitled, *I'd Push the Button,* before a national association of accountants. My title was taken from the first sentence: If there were a button on this podium, the pressing of which would return freedom immediately, I would *Push the Button.* To elaborate this point, I asked the audience to imagine that a big, burly ruffian had me on my back, hands around my neck, knees in my midriff. A dozen of my friends were looking on and bemoaning my plight, and I could hear their babble: "We must remove that ruffian but we must do it gradually or Read will get up and go to work all at once." I paraphrase the old saying about justice: Freedom delayed is freedom denied.

Most people say they are in favor of freedom, but reflect on the great number who deviate for a thousand and one reasons—ranging from the fear of competition to the lack of governmental subsidies to finance such pet projects. Cowards! Wrote Queen Elizabeth I: "Cowards falter, but danger is often overcome by *those who nobly dare!*"

Willful blindness is also an obstacle. "None are so blind as those who *will* not see." Everyone—no exception—is blind in more ways than he or she can count. But for my thesis, just one: Only now and then is there a citizen who is not blind to the way freedom works its wondrous ways. *Socialistic nonsense easily flows into a society afflicted by such emptyheadedness!*

"Men who know not their own path, yet point the way for others." What an astute observation! Millions who haven't the slightest idea of why they are alive and prosperous "know" they can point your and my way as to how we should live our lives. They use brute force—coercion—to achieve their ignoble non-sensical ways!

As gloomy as our situation appears, bear in mind that there are no hopeless situations. There are only individuals who feel hopeless. Let not their number cause us to predict a continuing failure. Wrote the English poet, John Keats (1795–1821): "Failure is, in a sense, the highway to success, inasmuch as every discovery of what is false leads us to seek earnestly after what is true, and every fresh experience points out some form of error which we shall afterward carefully avoid."

Wrote Thomas Jefferson: "Error of opinion may be tolerated where reason is left free to combat it." All obstacles to the good life are surmountable, providing we are free to speak and write about the wonders of freedom. The sure-fire remedy is to widen our door of perception. *Awake for freedom's sake!*

25

PERFECTION? KNOWING OUR IMPERFECTIONS

It is reasonable to have perfection in our eye that we may always advance toward it, though we know it can never be attained.
—SAMUEL JOHNSON

My schooling was skimpy. If my teachers ever mentioned Samuel Johnson (1709–84) the name left no lasting impression. My introduction came later.

In 1918 I was working as an airplane mechanic in Scotland. A friend and I were given a one-week pass and took a train for London. On the first day a cloudburst caused us to take refuge in a large library. There we met an American couple who had not been able to return to the States. We were the first U.S.A. soldiers they had seen and we were blest with their generosity. They hired a remarkable guide for us, who took us on a tour of the city. After five hours of gaping at London's wonders, we arrived at "Ye Old Cheshire Cheese" for luncheon—the restaurant made famous because Sam Johnson always lunched and dined there.

Afterward, our guide took us across the street to Johnson's old home. And there was the original English dictionary completed by Johnson in 1755. Every time I have been in London since that first visit I go to that unique restaurant and to Johnson's home.

The above quote which says *we know* that perfection can never be attained could easily be misunderstood. Who are the "we"? Johnson's scholarly self and a few others of similar intellectual rank. But no such modesty characterizes the millions of Englishmen and Americans of Johnson's time and ours, who have no question about their own near attainment of perfection!

Just as I began this brief essay, a news item came to my attention. It concerned a ruling by the City Council of one of our major cities that home Bible studies or worship meetings of *any kind* that include anyone not living in the home are illegal without a special use permit. The specious reasoning behind this edict is that such a meeting constitutes a religious service, which makes the home in which the service is held a church—in an area not zoned for a church!

Practical? No, fanatical! This ruling breaks not one but two of our hallowed traditions: one, it invades the privacy of the home; and two, it violates our freedom of worship. The political instigators of such legislation are as far from perfection as any dictator—utterly unaware of their imperfections!

Let this unawareness of imperfection go a step or two further and it will be illegal for an individual to say his prayers in private! Indeed, prayer is already against the law in ever so many schools! These politicos are so far from perfection that they are unaware of their know-nothing-ness. Thus, ignorance increasingly presides not only over their lives—unknowingly—but over the whole citizenry. The American philosopher, Ralph Barton Perry, wrote: "Ignorance deprives men of freedom because they do not know what alternatives there are. It is impossible to choose to do what one has never 'heard of'.''

The following are thoughts by several notable thinkers worthy of deep reflection:

- Ignorance of communism, Fabianism or any other police-state philosophy is far more dangerous than ignorance of the most virulent disease.
- Any frontal attack on ignorance is bound to fail because the masses are always ready to defend their most precious possession—their ignorance.
- It isn't the crook in modern business that we fear, but the honest man who doesn't know what he is doing.
- To be ignorant of one's ignorance is the malady of ignorance.
- Ignorance is not so damnable as humbug, but when it prescribes pills it may happen to do much harm.
- By ignorance is pride increased; those most assume who know the least.
- To be proud of learning is the greatest ignorance.
- Nothing is so haughty and assuming as ignorance where self-conceit sets up to be infallible.

There are two radically opposed concepts of government (1) The concept held by our Founding Fathers, which limited government to keeping the peace and invoking a common justice. This philosophy is all but forgotten except by a few. (2) The authoritarian concept of a government designed ''to exercise authority over; direct; control; rule; manage.'' This is the Command Society, which goes by a variety of labels ranging from serfdom to the police state. Millions of people in today's America are victims of the planned economy and various welfare state absurdities. Many of these victims would do a turnabout were there a realization that they are giving support to communism or Fabianism.

Frontal attacks—calling others ''ignorant'' or even thinking of them as ignoramuses is very injurious in two respects: (1) it hardens the condemned in their misconceptions and (2) it reveals an excessive proudness—vanity—in the name callers, an unawareness of *their own ignorance*. As Thomas Alva Edison said, ''No one knows more than one-millionth of one per cent of anything.''

''There is no need to fear the crook in today's business world,'' asserted the President of one of the world's largest corporations. It is a fact that swindlers in business are so easily discovered that they die aborning. Dishonesty, more often than not, causes customers to fade away before the police become aware that skulduggery is going on. Dishonest businessmen are not the real problem. Fear them not!

Should we, then, fear ''honest'' businessmen? Yes, because many businessman fall into this category and most of these— there are notable exceptions—know not what they do. Most businessmen, for example, are unaware of how the free market works its wonders, or even their contributions to its countless miracles. While personally they wouldn't steal a million dollars any more than a dime, they seek government aid to bail their operations out of bankruptcy, to thwart competition, to look after the poor with the fruits of your and my labor—stealing unknowingly!

To be ignorant of one's ignorance is, indeed, the malady of ignorance. I am unaware of any truth more difficult to communicate than this.

Were far more citizens than now aware of their ignorance— how infinitesimal their enlightenments—the freedom way of life would be the glorious reward!

Ignorance alone is bad enough, but it is not so damnable as humbug—ignorance put to evil uses. To humbug is ". . . to cheat, deceive, defraud." Humbuggery is dishonesty in action, which is about as far down in hellishness as man can go. It is ignorance to try to run other people's lives; it is humbuggery to prescribe fake remedies and trick pills for the havoc thus wrought. The resulting harm is what we are now witnessing—the destruction of a once free society. Wrote the English divine, Robert South (1634–1726): "All deception in the course of life is indeed nothing else but a lie reduced to practice, and falsehood passing from words into things."

"Those most assume who know the least." This aphorism ranks near topside as a description of those most guilty of societal depredations; this mentality is the source of plundering. The few individuals free of this ignorance know that running their own lives is the endless pursuit of intellectual, moral and spiritual righteousness. For those thus blest, the notion of running the lives of others, or plundering, is utter nonsense.

Another truth: "To be proud of learning is the greatest ignorance." Pride is: "exaggerated self-esteem, conceit." A very high percentage of Ph.D.'s, teachers, ordained clergymen and others, enamoured of their own "learning," haven't the slightest idea how freedom works its wonders. They are *proud* of their ignorance. Learned? Why, they don't even know that their notions are socialistic!

Where, when, and in whomsoever self-conceit sets up to be infallible we have another source of societal decadence. Wrote the English dramatist and editor, Douglas Jerrold (1803–57): "It is wonderful how near conceit is to insanity." I would substitute "tragic" for "wonderful."

Those who are admirers of themselves more than of virtue

think they are superior to others. To the contrary, their own attitude puts them on the lowest rung.

Dictocrats—those who run our lives—be they politicians, labor union leaders or whoever—and we have them by the millions—are victims of self-conceit. When enough of us see through their sham—much of it innocent—many of them will return to such virtue as is within their competence!

All of the above suggests what most know-it-alls would regard as comedy: Let's start a graduate college or university where, instead of awarding Ph.D.'s, only S.F.I.'s would be awarded: *Steps From Ignorance!* Seriously: Let's strike a blow for freedom: *De-regulate!*

26

GOOD NEWS

*Experience has convinced me that
there is a thousand times more
goodness, wisdom, and love in
the world than men imagine.*

How hard it is to imagine the existence of goodness, wisdom and love when quite the opposite is being drummed into our heads day in and day out. Television, press and radio emphasize the sordid, the bizarre, the ugly. Newscasters specialize in disaster. For one of countless examples, a DC-10 crash is headlined around the world. But who sees or hears mention of the millions of miles flown daily in safety!

The preponderance of bad news has a traumatic effect on those exposed to it. Millions of people are downcast, overwhelmed by gloom, seeing nothing ahead but disaster: murder, rape, mugging, vandalism, arson, armed robbery, theft or whatever.

This atmosphere of disaster tends to make us prophets of doom, stranded without hope, unable to see or imagine how freedom would work its wonders.

Reflect for a moment on some of the bad news about our country: rising prices and wages and interest rates, fuel and housing shortages, unemployment, unfavorable trade balances, higher health care costs, more welfare claimants, educational problems, mounting crime rates.

What we are being told by such headlines, if we'll only stop to ponder, is that coercive governmental intervention is bad news. Despite the good intentions of the proponents of easy money and credit, social security, Medicare, protectionism, subsidies to special interests, wage and price controls, more or different welfare programs—despite those good intentions the bad news is that each step of socialistic tampering leads inevitably to consequences that are undesirable. And the more burdensome and stifling the rules and regulations, the greater is the temptation to ignore or break such laws. This results in new demands upon government to cope with the consequences of the prior intervention. Bad news, compounded!

Now, think about that. Is it really bad news that coercive measures lead to undesirable consequences? No, not really. It would indeed be bad news if the consequences were anything else—if bad methods could be employed to yield good results. So, behind the "bad news" headlines on the state of the economy is the good news that socialism cannot deliver on its promises of something for nothing. There is an alternative, a better way, and that better alternative is freedom.

The *good news* concerns the private ownership and control of scarce and valuable resources and the voluntary exchange of goods and services in open competition—with government limited to keeping the peace and invoking a common justice. The *good news* is that we'll better serve ourselves and others when free to act creatively as each chooses. The *good news* is that coercion does diminish the resources and the productivity of everyone involved. So hail to the better way—freedom!

One of my favorite examples of good news appeared some time back in *The Ambassador* magazine:

- Last year more than 196,000,000 Americans were not arrested.

- More than 89,000,000 married persons did not file for divorce.

- More than 115,000,000 individuals maintained a formal affiliation with some religious group.

- More than 4,000,000 teachers and professors did not strike or participate in riotous demonstrations.

And then this brilliant and encouraging comment by the author: "Let those apostles of despair who preach hate and discord ask themselves what they have done and what they are doing for the good of their loved ones, their nation and the world."

Recently I read of a television station in Europe specializing in *reporting only the good news*. What a boon if all of us could tune to a "good news freedom station"—for those of us saturated with the bad news of violence and plunder are indeed hungering for the good news of freedom and its many blessings. What a viewer market such a station could profitably serve!

There was a time when the miracle of American productivity heralded good news around the world. Investigators came from many nations to seek the explanation. And none of these came closer to finding the right answer than did Alexis de Tocqueville when he visited here in the 1830s:

I sought for the greatness and genius of America in fertile

fields and boundless forests; it was not there. I sought for it in her free schools and her institutions of learning; it was not there. I sought for it in her matchless Constitution and democratic congress; it was not there. Not until I went to the churches of America and found them aflame with righteousness did I understand the greatness and genius of America. America is great because America is good. When America ceases to be good, America will cease to be great.[1]

Tocqueville read correctly the good news that the miracle of America was the outgrowth of the freedom of the individual. He knew, what so many today have forgotten, that such miracles are not attributable to the interventions and controls by those exercising political powers of coercion. He knew then, as we must learn anew today, that the coercive nature of overextended government is bad news.

As we reverse the tide—no longer captivated by the bad but anxious to learn more of the good—our America will move toward the good at an unbelievable rate. And the bad will rapidly fade away. Wrote the English poet, Oliver Goldsmith (1728–74): "Whatever mitigates the woes, or increases the happiness of others, is a just criterion of goodness; and whatever injures society at large, or any individual in it, is a criterion of iniquity."

The good news is that individuals best discover themselves and realize their potentialities when free. And thus do they contribute most to the good of their loved ones, their nation and the world.

---

[1]This quotation is found on pages 12–13 of the popular school text by F.A. Magruder, *American Government: A Textbook on the Problems of Democracy.* Except for the last two sentences, this is Magruder's paraphrase of Tocqueville's words.

NAME INDEX

Addison, 63, 81, 83, 96, 99
Aristippus, 63
Arrian, Flavius, 93
Augustine (Saint), 6
Aurelius, Marcus, 3, 6, 91
Austin, Henry, 77

Bastiat, Frederic, 59
Baxter, Richard, 16
Beecher, Henry Ward, 37, 71
Blair, Hugh, 49
Bovee, Christian, 64
Bradford, William, 36
Bulwer-Lytton, E. G., 68
Burke, Edmund, 5, 9, 20, 60,
    63, 72, 78, 84
Burleigh, Lord William, 22

Carlyle, Thomas, 68
Carruth, W. H., 66
Channing, Wm. E., 4, 29, 39
Chapin, Edwin H., 32, 70
Chesterfield, Philip, 68, 83
Chesterton, G. K., 9
Clark, James, 87
Cleveland, Grover, 53
Collyer, Robert, 80
Confucius, 69, 87
Cruden, Alexander, 76

Dickens, Charles, 44, 50
Dillaway, Newton, 95
Donne, John, 85
Dougall, Bernard, 40
Durant, Will, 8

Edison, Thomas A., 112
Edwards, Tryon, 28, 58, 63, 68,
    83, 97, 98
Elizabeth I, 108
Emerson, Ralph Waldo, 1, 13,
    33, 49, 76, 78, 85, 95
Emmons, Nathaniel, 50
Empedocles, 74
Epictetus, 90
Eulenberg-Wiener, Renee von,
    65
Evans, Mary Ann, 78

Foster, John, 63, 82
Franklin, Benjamin, 46
Fuller, Thomas, 26

Goethe, 27, 29, 46, 64, 77, 80
Goldsmith, Oliver, 84, 118
Goldthwaite, E. K., 82, 84, 118

Harvard, William, 5
Hawes, Joel, 67
Hazlitt, Henry, 96
Hazlitt, William, 29
Herrick, Robert, 78
Hill, Rowland, 84
Hubbard, Elbert, 60
Hunt, Leigh, 86
Hunter, John, 48

Jackson, Robert H., 6
James, 42, 43
Jefferson, Thomas, 108
Jerrold, Douglas, 113
Jesus, 45
John, 38
Johnson, Samuel, 64, 77, 109
Jordan, Virgil, 73
Jung, Carl, 72

Kant, Immanuel, 68, 84
Keats, John, 108
Kemmerer, Donald, 22
Keynes, John Maynard, 23
Kingsley, Charles, 84
Kossuth, Louis, 84
Krummacher, Frederich, 44
Kunkel, Fritz, 28, 72

Lawrence, David H., 45
Leo, III (Pope), 59
Lewis, C. S., 51
Lincoln, Abraham, 5
Longfellow, H. W., 25
Lowell, James Russell, 67

McKay, Charles, 89

Mallet, David, 32
Mann, Horace, 48
March, Daniel, 3
Mason, John M., 89
Matthew, 41, 82
Milton, John, 30, 32, 40
Montaigne, 39
Morley, Felix, 9
Munger, Theodore T., 28, 68

Newman, Cardinal J. H., 24
Noüy, Pierre Lecomte du, 66

Opitz, Edmund, 73

Paine, Thomas, 105
Pascal, Blaise, 3
Penn, William, 71, 103
Perry, Ralph Barton, 110
Peter (I), 31
Potter, D. F., 63

Punshon, William Morley, 69

Quarles, Francis, 68

Raleigh, Walter, 70
Reuther, Walter, 18
Richter, Jean Paul, 81
Robin Hood, 35
Rowe, Nicholas, 26
Ruskin, John, 77, 106
Russell, Bertrand, 49

Sarpi, Paolo, 59
Seneca, 10
Shakespeare, 6, 29, 43, 88
Shelley, Percy B., 70
Simms, William, 77
Smith, Adam, 72
Sockman, Ralph, 75
Socrates, 75
South, John, 22, 113
Spanheim, Frederick, 47
Spencer, Herbert, 29, 55, 84
Sprague, William, 32
Spurgeon, Charles H., 62
Standen, Anthony, 92
Swetchine, Madam, 84
Swift, Jonathan, 50, 71

Taylor, Jeremy, 79
Thoreau, Henry David, 23, 32
Tocqueville, 80, 117–118
Trublet, Nicholas, 64

Walton, Izaak, 99
Washington, George, 69, 72
Weisenburger, Walter, 7
White, Andrew D., 59, 88
White, Stewart Edward, 60, 83
Wordsworth, William, 34